A D A

KU-410-392

Quebec

Montreal

Ottawa

ST LAWRENCE

MAINE

MINNE-
OTA

Lake Superior

MICHIGAN

WISCONSIN

Lake Huron

Minneapolis

MI-
CHI-
GAN

Toronto

Lake Ontario

NEW HAMPSHIRE

VERMONT

Boston

Lake Michigan

Lake Erie

NEW YORK

Hudson R.

MASSA-
CHUSETS

Milwaukee

RHODE
ISLAND

MTS.

CONNEC-
TICUT

Chicago

IOWA

INDI-

OHIO

PENNSYLVANIA

DELAWARE RIVER

NEW JERSEY

Mississippi R.

New York
Philadelphia
Baltimore

Pittsburg

ILLINOIS

Missouri R.

MIS-

ANA

OHIO R.

Cincinnati

WEST

POTOMAC R.

DELAWARE

VIRGI-

MARYLAND

NIAI

Washington

Kansas
City

St Louis

KENTUCKY

VIRGINIA

SOURI

TENNESSEE R.

APPALACHIAN

NORTH

OMA

ARKANSAS

TENNESSY RIVER

CAROLINA

Memphis

ARKANSAS R.

SOUTH

MISSISSIPPI R.

CAROLINA

ARKANSAS

MISSIS-

Atlanta

RED R.

SIPPI

ALABAMA

GEORGIA

Houston

LOUISIANA

New Orleans

Galveston

FLORIDA

A T L A N T I C   O C E A N

Miami

G U L F   O F   M E X I C O

0	50	100	200	300	MILES
0	100	200	300	400	500 KLMS.

LIFE IN MODERN AMERICA

Peter Bromhead, M.A., D.Phil.
Professor of Politics, University of Bristol

Life in Modern America

Longman

LONGMAN GROUP LIMITED
London

Associated companies, branches and representatives
throughout the world

© Longman Group Limited 1970
First published 1970
New impressions, 1971, 1972 (*twice*), 1973

ISBN 0 582 52642 6

Printed in Great Britain by Butler & Tanner Ltd
Frome and London

Contents

Acknowledgements

We would like to thank the following for permission to reproduce the illustrations:

Ray Hamilton, Camera Press Limited for p. 98, bottom; The John Hillelson Agency Limited for p. 136; 151, bottom; Mississippi Cooperative Extension Service for p. 151, top; The Museum of Modern Art, New York, Philip Johnson Fund for p. 203, top; The National Aeronautics and Space Administration for p. 15; United Press International for p. 81; 127, bottom; 182; 203, bottom; 227; United States Information Service for p. 2; 48; 74; 98, top; 112; 127, top; 160; 169, top; 187; 196; 212; 227; 232; United States Travel Service for p. 20.

Introduction

There is one thing about which almost all modern men agree: that technological progress is good—good not just for its own sake but for the sake of the greater comfort, security, leisure and variety of experience that it makes possible, not just for a privileged few but for the great mass of people. No society has yet eliminated poverty, slums and starvation, but material progress alone can provide the conditions for such an achievement. All the world looks to North America, and particularly to the United States, as that part of the world which has been most successful in producing widespread material wealth combined with political freedom. The lead of the United States in all this is so widely recognised that most people tend to describe it as 'America', forgetting Canada and the whole of Latin America.

There is not the same agreement about the values and social organisation on which this progress has been based. American achievements in material progress have led the world, but the world's admiration is mixed with envy, and with disapproval, more or less intense, of the competitive methods by which the progress has been gained. Some think that collective action is a morally better and more efficient method than a sum total of individual and self-regarding actions by great numbers of people competing with one another for pre-eminence. Some see America as harsh, selfish and materialistic, and there are critics in America too. But most Americans have no doubt about their allegiance to the individualist idea. They have been ready to modify and mellow its practical effects here and there, just as collectivist societies are now leaving more room for the individual; but Americans see their achievements and their failures (such as the proliferating violence and crime), as the product of their long-accepted values. In economic life there is not equality of possessions, but there is a good measure of equality of opportunity; in social life there is equality of consideration; in politics the people have good means of choosing those who are to have authority, and of controlling them and limiting their power.

This book will try to present a picture of American society and life as it is in the late 1960s. It is hoped that it will be useful for students, mainly in Europe, but also in other parts of the world, who wish to acquaint themselves with the main problems that confront Americans at this time, and with the way in which they handle these problems.

Many writers have in the past attempted to portray America, and some of those who are now read were European. There still remains the great classic *Democracy in America* by Alexis de Tocqueville based on a visit to the United States in the early 1830s—still rewarding for the depth of its understanding not only of American society in its day but of the underlying trends and qualities which have continued up to the present. Few works have been produced with such prophetic elements: De Tocqueville saw the trend towards conformity in current fashions which arose both from the lack of long-established traditions and from the search for values to remedy this. He saw too the importance of allegiance to small groups within the society as a corrective against the danger of tyranny by the mass. Any book which tries to see America as it is even in the modern age must look back at this great work of 130 years ago. There were other Europeans in the nineteenth century who produced works of great insight, but it is perhaps hardly useful to give a list of these here.

Among more recent surveys on America two books are worth citing. Gabriel Almond wrote *The American People and Foreign Policy* in 1950, and here the author moves on from de Tocqueville and his other predecessors to some useful summaries of the nature of American society and its values. Ten years later another political scientist, S. M. Lipset, wrote *The First New Nation*. Here too we find insights of great value for an understanding of American society. Lipset's book is more directed to political scientists and uses some of the rather complex concepts and definitions of modern sociologists and political scientists.

One difficulty for a student of American society today is that he is confronted by a mass of literature so vast that it cannot be comprehended. Never has any society been engaged in so much inquiry about itself. The mass of information about attitudes, beliefs, values, the economic situation and feelings towards money is so immense that almost any question about the people can be answered by reference to the results of some survey or report. The government itself produces a marvellous stream of statistical information. Where de Tocqueville relied on insight the modern writer's task is to try to make a fair selection from the mass of facts which have been discovered, analysed and presented. One difficulty arising from this mass of literature is that it is becoming more and more technical, and less and less easily understood by the ordinary untrained reader. The approach to the subject in this book is based on an assumption that readers are unfamiliar with the technical language which has been developed by sociologists as they talk to one another, and it may suffer somewhat in precise accuracy because of this.

The approach is first to look at the background of the country and at the people—where they came from, how they went to America and what they have done since they went there. Much attention is paid to immigration and to movement within the United States, to the form of government and to the shape of political life. From this we move to an attempt to understand the current social and economic problems, with special attention to the difficulties that arise from relations between the different races.

In the picture of modern America education is an element of which the importance should not be underestimated. For this reason the study of education concentrates in particular on the advanced stages at universities and similar institutions, which are now influencing the whole economic and social structure to an extent never seen before. Religion too is a subject which is peculiar in its American setting; in Europe scientific progress and economic advance have in general been accompanied by a decline in the influence of religion, but in America there is little sign of any such development. Religion is only one aspect of

private life, and other aspects are dealt with too. In such a big
country communications deserve attention too. Finally a chapter
about America in its relation to the world sums up the whole of
the political and social system as it sees itself, as it is seen by
others, and as it looks outwards on the world outside.

This book is based partly on experience of living in America,
partly on continuing contacts with Americans in England,
partly on the reading of the current American literature about
the society. The subject is so vast that no author can claim with
any assurance to have selected wisely from all that could be
offered. The attempt here is to select those features which seem
of particular significance and which reveal the obvious
differences between America and Europe, showing how this
great new culture has developed in directions different from
those of the cultures out of which it originally grew.

I should like to acknowledge my indebtedness to the works
of S. M. Lipset and G. A. Almond in particular among living
writers; to the numerous publications of the United States
Government and of the United States Information Service; to
many people with whom I have discussed the work, or who have
read all or part of it, notably Professor Robert Zimmer of the
University of Minnesota and Dean Hopkins of the University of
Massachusetts; to Stephen Cooksey for his most valuable help
in gathering information; and to Christina Shell and Valerie
Hayward for typing and retyping the manuscript. Meanwhile, I
am myself responsible for all the errors of fact and emphasis that
may be observed.

CHAPTER ONE

Atlantic to Pacific

Desert land in New Mexico

New York skyline

1. A Single Culture

In its vast area the United States comprehends most of the
physical conditions known to men; heat and cold, forest and
desert, tropical swamp and Arctic waste, mountains and endless
plains, empty spaces and megalopolis, and the world's largest
river system. Yet the most remarkable contrast of all is the
contrast between the variety inevitable in so great an area and
the similarity of the people and of the things that they have
made in all these diverse parts.

The United States is bigger in area than the whole of Europe,
and includes a spread as great as from Paris to Karachi in
Pakistan. Evidently life in the hot southern sub-tropical forests
is very different from life in the north, where the winters are
colder than anywhere in western Europe.

It would not be easy to talk in general terms about western
Europe as a unit, with its differences of climate and culture, its
mountains, plains and coasts. One would have to describe the
various parts one by one, and it would take a long time to do so.
In the far bigger area of the United States, with far greater
diversity of climate, there are also contrasts: there are too many
characteristics to be described in a single generalisation. And
the diversity of the people themselves is immense: it is not only
that some came originally from Britain, others from Italy,
Germany, Ireland or Poland; first-generation immigrants are
still close to their diverse origins, while most long-established
Americans are wholly assimilated; first-generation Italians
differ not only from long-established Dutch, but from fourth-
generation Italians—and even they differ according to the
degree of intermarriage. Yet there is at the same time a lack

3

of cultural difference among the regions, because all these varied peoples are scattered everywhere, with only minor local ethnic concentrations.

The great Republic of the United States is not the same country, even in area, as it was at the time of its foundation in the 1780s. The original Union consisted of thirteen states along the eastern seaboard. The thirty-five continental states which have been added since independence occupy an area eight times as great as the original thirteen, and more than two-thirds of all Americans now live in these thirty-five states, in an area which 180 years ago was mainly unexplored, except for some Spanish and French coastal settlements here and there. But the founders of the Constitution foresaw that, as settlement spread westwards and new areas were developed by stable populations capable of self-government, so new states would be allowed to join the Union. The process began almost at once. Kentucky and Tennessee, southwards and across the mountains from Virginia, were added in 1792 and 1796, and further north the admission of states west of Pennsylvania began with Ohio in 1803.

The story of the addition of new states in the nineteenth century is also the story of the conquest of the west, with the wagons and then the railroads, the cowboys and the sheriffs and that piece of human experience which the Western movie constantly revives. The last block of north-western states was not incorporated until after 1890. With Arizona in 1912 the list of forty-eight continental states was at last complete, and recently, in 1959, the first separate territories were granted statehood—Hawaii in the Pacific Ocean and the great northern pioneers' land of Alaska, bigger than France, Germany, Italy and Austria together—and still with only a quarter of a million people.

The story of the growth of the Union reminds us that within the United States there is a difference between old and new. To Europeans America may look a new country, but it is not all new in the same way. Even in Europe, apart from churches and castles, there is not so very much left from more than 200 years ago. Houses, shops, factories, stores, means of transport—almost all the buildings and the things people use are less old than the United States. From four million at the time of independence the population there has grown to 200 million, but this does not mean that all parts have grown at the same rate. The State of Virginia now has six times as many people as in 1787, but modern England has five times as many as it had then. If we exclude the part of Virginia which consists of suburbs of Washington, we find a rate of increase about the same as in England itself over this period. In most aspects of everyday life, Virginia is not really newer than the mother country. But with the western states things are quite different. There, hardly anything man-made goes back 100 years, and few adult inhabitants have roots going back more than one generation. So there is a contrast within the United States between old and new, less obvious than many other contrasts but significant and interesting all the same.

Although the country is so big and its people have so many different ethnic backgrounds, it is in some ways less varied than Europe. The national origins of the people are by now fairly well mixed all over the country, though there are exceptions on small and large scales. The English language is virtually universal in its American form. The American way of speaking has developed independently of England and is on the whole closer to what can be heard in Ireland than to the speech of any other part of the British Isles. Regional variations of accent are slight, and to a German or an Italian the difference between the accent of the deep south and that of the 'Yankee' is less evident than the difference between two Englishmen from places two hours' journey apart. Some Americans speak rather indistinctly, not pronouncing consonants properly, others show by their speech that English is not their mother tongue, and Irish or Negro accents can often be recognised; but the lack of real regional or class variety in speech or usage is one of the characteristics that tend to make the whole country very obviously one.

Another instance of uniformity is in habits and ways of living. From Boston to Los Angeles is as far as from France to Central Asia, and from east to west there are five time zones; but everywhere people get up and go to bed at about the same time, eat the same kind of food, bought in the same kind of shops, work and rest at the same times of the day and have the same pattern of holidays. In general they share the same ideas, ideals and objectives. In most of the things that matter there is

less difference between rich people and ordinary people, or
between town and country, than in any single European nation.
It is fairly easy to imagine a typical American; most individuals
deviate from this 'type' in some ways, but are fairly near to it
in others. It is not that this personal uniformity is boring. It is
after all superimposed on an original diversity, and where the
single pattern involves much friendly informality in personal
relations there is little cause to feel oppressed.

Although the United States covers so much land and the land
produces far more food than the present population needs, its
people are by now almost entirely an urban society. Less than a
tenth of the people are engaged in agriculture and forestry, and
most of the rest live in or around towns, small and large. Here
the traditional picture is changing; every small town may still
be very like other small towns, and the typical small town may
embody a widely accepted view of the country, but most
Americans do not live in small towns any more. Half the
population now live in some thirty metropolitan areas (large
cities with their suburbs) of more than a million people each—
a larger proportion than in Germany or England, let alone
France—and if we add another 200 or so quite large towns with
their suburbs we see that the small town has been superseded
by the large town as the typical environment—or, to be more
exact, by the suburban section of a large town. The statistics of
urban and rural population should be treated with caution,
because so many people who live in areas classified as rural
travel by car to work in a nearby town each day. As the rush
to live out of town continues rural areas within reach of towns
are gradually filled with houses, so that it is hard to say at what
moment a piece of country becomes a suburb. But more and
more the typical American lives in a metropolitan rather than a
small town environment—with no single metropolis to dominate
the rest, no magnet to compare with Paris or London, Moscow
or Tokyo; every great city shares in a single metropolitan
quality.

The fact that the United States has always been a single
economic unit, with no tariffs to restrict trade, has contributed
to uniformity. Modern industry favours large organisations, and
it is no accident that the world's biggest commercial firms are
American. Mass-markets are efficient; the constituent pieces are

interchangeable. The people are interchangeable too. They can choose between the products of competing manufacturers, but the products are all much alike. The air-conditioners and the machines for washing clothes and dishes, the smooth-running automatic super-comfortable car, the one-storey house in its pleasant piece of land, with its plate-glass windows and its swimming pool—all these things are good, but each has many others like it, just as there are too many car-parks and garages and signs about things for sale. The different parts and communities of the United States are like one another in the same way as big airports all over the world are like one another— and after all mass air travel developed in America before it did anywhere else. Except, up to a point, in the south, there is not much really distinctive regional architecture or cookery, music or literature. This is why Americans are so impressed by a Mediterranean fishing port or hilltop town.

2. The Main Regions

North America belongs to people who came there across the Atlantic, most from Europe, some as slaves from Africa. So when we look at this vast country there is good reason for beginning with the east coast, where the first and later immigrants landed. Beginning with the north we have first the area known as New England, which runs from the Canadian shore to New York, with a coastline 800 kilometres long (in direct line) and stretching inland for 500 kilometres at its widest point. This area is about the same size as England and Wales, and resembles old England in many ways. Some of the earliest settlement was here, and on the whole the country is small-scale, long established and urban. In character we can divide New England roughly into two parts. The southern section, consisting of the states of Connecticut, Massachusetts and Rhode Island, is the most 'English'. The ten million people of these states are as crowded as the English, and most live in towns—a quarter of them in and round Boston and another fifth (or nearly so) in the outer parts of the great sprawl that runs up the coast from New York City. Boston already had a quarter of a million people 100 years ago, and in its central part many streets are well over 100 years old. In this old-established part

the scenery is rather English, with flat country near the coast
and hills up to 1,000 metres inland.

Northern New England is rather different, emptier, wilder,
more picturesque. The states of Maine, New Hampshire and
Vermont together have only two million people in an area as
big as England. The southern parts of New Hampshire and
Maine are suburban, but everywhere else, with lakes and hills
up to 1,300 metres in Vermont, spectacular rocky coasts in
Maine, this is more than anything an attractive holiday country
for the town-dwellers further south: country for enjoyments
like yachting, swimming, fishing, skiing and enjoying rural
peace—particularly in the 'fall' (autumn), when the colours
are glorious.

The south end of New England merges into the suburbs of
New York City, and to the west the great state that takes its
name from the city at its southernmost tip. Some say that New
York is the world's biggest 'town', but it is rather pointless to
argue whether or not it is bigger than Tokyo. It all depends
how many areas which are more or less attached are included.
Manhattan Island includes everything that most people think
of when they say 'New York': Wall Street and the office sky-
scrapers clustered around it, Fifth Avenue running up the
centre of the island, with Broadway slanting from it, the Empire
State Building, Rockefeller Centre, the United Nations Building,
the museums and central shops, Central Park (where at times
it is dangerous to walk alone), the Negro quarter of Harlem, the
docks and the slums behind them; but Manhattan has only
around two million residents. New York City is composed of
five boroughs: Manhattan, Brooklyn (on the south of Long
Island), the Bronx, Richmond and Queen's. Immense bridges
join the boroughs with each other and with the suburbs in New
Jersey across the Hudson. The city population of nearly eight
million has not changed much for a long time, but the area of
continuous town can be taken to include in addition about
seven million people in New York State, New Jersey and
southern Connecticut, bringing the total to about fifteen million.

Eastern New York State is really the same thing as the valley
of the Hudson River, but the State extends 500 kilometres to the
west to Lakes Ontario and Erie and Canada, and finally Niagara
Falls. The state is as big as England. Half of its seventeen

million people live in New York City, while the rest are mainly
concentrated in the line of Hudson valley towns and near the
Great Lakes, leaving much of the hill and lake country empty.
It has sometimes been argued that New York City might as well
be a state on its own. To the south of the state is Pennsylvania,
which also spreads out to the borders of the middle west, with
well-separated areas of coal mining and heavy industry among
its hills. Philadelphia, well up the Delaware River, is the
metropolis of Pennsylvania, with four million people in its
'metropolitan area', or city plus suburbs. In the western part of
the state the steel area around Pittsburgh is already across the
mountains and on the Ohio River; water flows south to the
Gulf of Mexico. Pennsylvania is the main part of the mid-
Atlantic area, which includes New Jersey and Maryland,
bounded at the south by the Potomac River. This is the clearest
dividing-line in the United States, because across the river is
the south.

It was on this border that the founding fathers chose the site
for the national capital city of Washington. They set apart for
it a square territory which they called the District of Columbia,
taken out of the states of Maryland and Virginia to form the
national capital territory, outside the jurisdiction of any state
and subject only to the control of the Federal Congress.

The whole of New England and the mid-Atlantic states
together can conveniently be regarded as a single section of the
United States, comprising eleven states together with the
District of Columbia. This is the base from which America was
built, and it still has a third of the whole population, in one-
fifteenth of the land area.

The north-east as a whole is slightly smaller than France in
area but larger in population. More than half of its fifty-five
million people are concentrated in the coastal area of early
settlement. The train from Boston through Providence, New
York, Philadelphia and Baltimore to Washington travels
between buildings for most of the way, and the part from
Philadelphia to New York, and a good way beyond in each
direction, is almost solidly built up. With good roads and
universal car ownership each of the big cities in this string
spreads out its suburbs towards its neighbour, and people talk
of this as megalopolis.

It hardly seems sensible to talk of Boston and Washington as parts of a single urban complex, when they are 600 kilometres apart, but this area contains the political capital of the United States as well as the commercial capital and most of the established centres of culture.

On southwards down the Atlantic coast are the tobacco and cotton states, with Washington on the border between south and north. This was slave-owning country before the civil war, and has not prospered much since then. Economically these south-eastern states are notoriously backward, with much rural poverty surviving among whites as well as negroes; more recently they have attracted a great new wave of industrial development, helped by federal plans and hydro-electric power.

Rather different from the rest of the south is its most extreme part, the state of Florida, with its swamps and pine forests, its orange plantations, its beaches, inland springs and waterways in a Caribbean climate. Miami, near the southern tip of the mainland, is perhaps America's best known holiday resort, with its row of immense hotels along its shores. But it is also a growing centre of prosperous new industries, and its metropolitan area population has surpassed the two traditional capitals of the south, Atlanta and New Orleans.

Behind and through the eastern states runs the range of the Appalachian mountains, beginning far south in Georgia and continuing, with slight interruptions, northwards to Vermont and Canada. Sections of the range have different names, but the different parts have much in common. Rounded hills and forests are the main feature. The highest point is only 2,000 metres above the sea.

The mountains were a barrier to early movement westwards for the early generations, but beyond the mountains the vast central plain stretches all the way to the Rocky Mountains, with the water from the Ohio and Missouri Rivers joining the Mississippi to flow down to New Orleans and the Gulf of Mexico. Half the area of the United States lies in this vast basin bounded by the Appalachians on the east and the Rocky Mountains to the west, with, to the north, the scarcely perceptible watershed which divides the Mississippi waters from those that flow north into the Great Lakes and St Lawrence. The north-eastern part of this area is occupied by five heavily populated states, Ohio, Michigan, Indiana, Illinois and Wisconsin, all bordering the Great Lakes, but all (except Michigan) including parts of the Ohio–Mississippi basins. Chicago is long-established as the metropolis, but now its stockyards, and the agriculture that made them famous, are overshadowed by the industry all round. With forty million people in an area a little greater than France this region's farms, though still important, occupy only a small part of the population. Half the people live in a dozen big cities or their suburbs. There are great open spaces, but the factories are never very far away.

The three states across the Mississippi River, Minnesota, Iowa and Missouri, are more predominantly farming areas, though with some big cities. The term 'mid-west' covers all these eight states. Although their agriculture is still a major source of wealth, industry and urban life have become pre-dominant, and there are nine metropolitan areas of over a million people each.

Further west still the great plain which occupies the middle of the United States from Canada down to Texas is empty, featureless country, where one can drive for hours with little change of scene, and where the vastness of America is palpable. The plains run from the Gulf of Mexico in the south up to the Canadian border and beyond—an endless open space comparable with Siberia. Few places in the world can compare with these great plains for uniformity and monotony, and they are only part of a continuous system which goes northwards to the barren lands of the Arctic. The eastern part has a moderate rainfall, but in general the rainfall declines towards the mountain barrier of the Rockies in the west. Although there are great extremes of cold in winter and of heat in summer the plains are more favourably placed than those of Siberia. Running from thirty to forty-nine degrees north they can produce wheat in large quantities, and the endless space is good for the use of mechanisation on a huge scale. One can well imagine the sense of isolation of the early settlers in this region, but the new developments of road transport have changed all this for the modern farmer. The four states forming the heart of the plains, North and South Dakota, Nebraska and Kansas, have a combined area nearly as great as France and Italy together, and only five million inhabitants including those who live in and around the two big cities on the Missouri river, which forms the extra boundary.

At the southern end of the plains is the huge state of Texas, largest in the Union until surpassed in size by the addition of sub-arctic and arctic Alaska. Texas is relatively arid, and has always had a distinctive quality, first with its cowboys and cattle, then with the rapid development of oil and industry. The population is growing fast and has now surpassed that of Pennsylvania, making Texas the third most populous state in the Union, but most of the state is still empty, with the people concentrated in a few big cities, famous for their millionaires, their brashness and their violence.

To the west the plains merge into rising land, the cattle country of the old wild west, the Rocky Mountains and the great deserts, much emptier yet than the plains. An area as big as Europe has fewer people than the Netherlands. Yet in some of these deserted areas, such as the states of Arizona, New Mexico and Nevada, we can now see new jobs multiplying and new inhabitants pouring in. Some of these areas have had ups and downs in the past, mostly because of some spectacular gold rush which produced a sudden boom town, now deserted. Nevada had nearly as many people in 1880 as in 1920, after some fluctuations, but the population has quintupled in the last thirty years.

The desert states have boom towns again, and the boom is not based only on unrestricted gambling or easy divorce laws. Being easily accessible to California is an advantage, and with their remarkable scenery they have obvious attractions for holidaymakers. They can still identify themselves with the old wild west, at the same time as they give conducted tours of canyons and breath-taking shapes of mountain and rock under ever-blue skies. For all their newness these areas represent a little of the American's image of his country. Here the frontier seems real, and in a sense it is, though now mixed with air-conditioning.

But for the fullest, most significant representation of the modern American image we must go to the Pacific coast and to the southern part of it in particular. Steinbeck's Okies in *The Grapes of Wrath,* driven out of the dust-bowl land of

Oklahoma, saw this as the promised land because of the hope
of some work picking fruit. But now it is not just oranges that
bring people west, nor just Hollywood. Roaring, fast-growing
America has its centrepiece here, and each year half a million
people are joining the search for the Californian dream.
Glorious mountains, sea with majestic cliffs as well as inviting
expanses of sand, scenery which leaves the east coast and the
mid-west looking very dull by comparison, warm winters,
sunshine, the world's biggest trees (Redwoods) these are only
part of the story. The oranges and grapes and fertile land are
still important, but the electronics industry, aeroplane factories,
defence plants of many kinds, and a whole new industrial
complex are more important still. The trouble is that southern
California is being ruined by its own success. In what was
once the best area of all, around Los Angeles, there will soon
be ten million people in one continuous urban development
100 kilometres across; and there are more motor-cars than in
the whole of Asia and the Soviet Union. Northern California,
with San Francisco as its centre, is less brash, more sensitive,
its people less prone to follow political or religious extremists
or cranks. Some people even think the state should be split in
two.

Surprisingly, the northern Pacific states of Washington and
Oregon, which only became states in 1889, have not progressed
as rapidly as California, although they too, like British
Columbia, have everything in their favour. It is not that they
are not prosperous; rather that they are just above the average
for the whole country in wealth and population-growth and
general dynamism. With their immense natural advantages they
are likely to shoot ahead very soon, and to take the mountain
states of Wyoming and Idaho with them.

In all this western part, although fruit-growing was the first
activity and is still immensely flourishing, life is mainly urban,
based on specialised industries demanding high-level skill and
training. In the far west everything man-made is new, and
although, as everywhere else, city streets and suburban houses
look much the same as in all the rest of the United States, the
newness belongs unquestionably here. This is a land made by
modern man for his enjoyment, although the process brings
unpleasant features with it, such as a crime rate double the

national average. But without the west modern America would not be complete; both geographically and sentimentally there is a sense in which it all leads out to California.

California has one place whose fame goes back to the early days of the great rush to prosperity and growth: Hollywood. No institution has ever before been such an instrument for conveying images and myths about any one country to every corner of the world. There must be few people anywhere who have not seen America's past and present represented in films and television serials. The picture may be partly false or misleading, with too much emphasis on crime and violence: but however much one may criticise the mass media of entertainment, it is appropriate that they started in California and have grown up with it. Hollywood has a good claim to interpret America to the world, because it is in the place where all American civilisation is distilled into an image of its own destiny.

3. Climate

The climate of the United States is extremely varied, and in some ways hostile. One thing that people tend to forget is how far south even the northern parts of the United States are in comparison with western Europe. New York is on about the same parallel of latitude as Naples in Italy, Boston and Detroit are no further north than Rome or Barcelona. (Even Toronto in Canada is further south than Marseilles.) In all of the heavily populated parts of the United States the summer can be exceedingly hot, and particularly near the eastern seaboard it is very unpleasant. In the great cities a tremendous heat is built up, made more disagreeable by high humidity. The inhabitants do not like discomfort, and have developed advanced techniques to make summer life tolerable; air-conditioning is one of the symbols of a home or office or factory that is based on reasonable economic success. It is very desirable indeed to have an air-conditioned interior.

In the winter on the other hand it can be very cold. Particularly away from the coast the winter cold is so intense that strong heating systems are essential if normal life is to be carried on. Even near the east coast in New York and Boston

The United States (on the left of the picture) seen from the Apollo 8 spacecraft

there are some spells of very cold weather indeed, though these
may be interspersed with much milder weather. Short term
fluctuations of remarkable violence are very common, so that
within a short period people must adapt themselves from almost
arctic conditions to something very like the normal summer,
shortly varied again to cold weather.

On the west coast the climate is much more equable. One of
the great advantages of California is that there are no extremes.
Except in the desert the summer is never intolerably hot, and
the winter is mild. The coastal region suffers from much mist
and drizzle, though only a little way inland the weather is
commonly very much clearer. Inland from California Arizona
and New Mexico can produce some of the highest temperatures
of any inhabited part of the globe. Modern air-conditioning
techniques have made life in these areas tolerable and even
agreeable where until not very long ago it was almost beyond
human endurance.

Much of America suffers a certain insecurity from violent
climatic happenings. Best known of these are the hurricanes
which afflict the south-east, particularly during the autumn.
Originating in the Caribbean these circular storms tend to move
north-eastwards, and any part of the deep south is liable to find
itself in the track of a particular hurricane. In general it is the
areas nearest to the coasts which suffer most severely. There
are certain to be several hurricanes each autumn, though they
do not all follow the same course. Some of them maintain their
strength far up into the north, and may cause severe damage
in areas as far north as New York. But some autumns pass
without anything very serious happening, and although every
south-eastern coastal place risks damage at some time, it has
some chance of remaining unscathed for years together.

Human ingenuity has not yet found any means of mitigating
the damage which hurricanes may cause to buildings and
property in general. Curiously, people have shown themselves
quite ready to build houses in areas which are particularly
subject to danger from hurricanes, and sometimes thousands of
expensive new houses are destroyed within a short time of being
built. On the other hand skills in weather prediction are well
advanced. Each hurricane is called by a girl's name, and its
path and force can be predicted long enough for people to be

warned in time to protect themselves, or to escape from danger in good time. Many severe hurricanes have caused much material damage but no loss of life. So the dangers of living in a hurricane zone seem acceptable when compared with the other dangers which have to be faced every day.

Much of the mid-west is similarly subject to damage from violent wind storms, here commonly called 'tornadoes'. As in the south-west damage is often extensive, but the likelihood of any particular place suffering from a tornado is very slight. There are several dozens of tornadoes each year, but each is short-lived and localised, likely to cause devastation in a restricted area. On the other hand, tornadoes are less easy to predict than south-eastern hurricanes, and they are more likely to cause death or injury to people, and to cause particularly severe suffering over small areas.

Another problem of the eastern half of the United States behind the Appalachian Mountains, in the whole basin of the Mississippi, Missouri and Ohio rivers, is the danger of flood. Severe storms and heavy rainfall can raise the level of these rivers to dangerous heights. In the history of the United States river floods have probably caused more damage than any other single climatic element. Enormous resources have been devoted to flood control, and in the spring of 1969 exceptional amounts of snow melted without disaster.

The great plains of the middle west where wheat is grown in vast quantities correspond more closely with conditions found in southern Russia than with anything in western Europe. In winter cold and wind are particularly intense, and the pioneers had to suffer considerable hardships before they had established enough comfort to give them reasonable shelter. But the modern mechanised farmer has little to fear provided that his equipment functions as it should.

In the Rocky Mountains the climate is what would be expected in a mountain area, with heavy snow in winter matched by brilliant sunshine and warm days in the summer even up to quite considerable heights. The mountains seem to have an enormous prospect as a holiday area, and vast sections of them have not yet been opened up. Here too the problem of what to do with the water has been acute, and enormous schemes already exist for controlling it and for deriving electric power from the great flow of waters in the Colorado and other great rivers.

The climate of the United States, with all its variations and violence—its frost and snow reaching far into the south, and the great heat of summer—made life difficult for the ill-equipped pioneers and for the Indians before them. But now so much of life goes on in the shelter of buildings that most people can carry on their lives without much concern for what is going on outside. Already some architects favour structures without windows; but it may be some time yet before American man turns his back on the weather altogether.

CHAPTER TWO

The People and their Origins

An Indian camp

Fifth Avenue, New York

1. The Beginnings

How often do we hear people say that America has no history, or not much of it? This is a false opinion that must be quickly removed if we are to understand the modern nation. There is indeed no American Louis XIV, no Richelieu, no Henry VIII; no Napoleon, no Bismarck, no Potemkin; no long record of foreign wars; American school children can hardly be asked to look back at any great national military hero to revere. Washington and Lincoln, and the Revolution and Civil War, are sometimes used to fill this unimportant gap. The Revolution was not really a revolution as far as the Americans were concerned; for them it was only an episode by which they cut the surviving political links with their far-off homeland; links which were already no more than a trivial encumbrance, interfering slightly in the process of their own development. The Civil War, which they fought among themselves after nearly a hundred years of independence, was indeed an important stage in the history of the technology of war; it taught a lesson to the world in general —that for success in war skilful leadership and courageous fighting qualities were not enough unless supported by industrial power. For the Americans in particular it merely confirmed a well-established principle that had just been challenged for the first time: that the United States formed a single nation—though it also created resentments that still survive.

The things that really matter in American history are not wars and major events of this kind; what matters is the process by which first hundreds, then thousands, then millions of people built their own society, developed the natural resources of their country, and produced a political system which has been not only stable and resilient but also tolerant and able to stimulate and respond to very substantial, constructive and genuine self-criticism.

It is only partly true to say that French history belongs to the French people, English to the English people. Their history (or that part of it which children learn at school, and which influences their thinking) is mainly the story of the actions and interactions of rulers and great men. More recently the ordinary people have developed a significance of their own, less controlled from above, less passive, less alienated. In Europe this process has involved revolutionary change. But in American history the ordinary people have been the most significant actors from the very beginning. America's past belongs to all the people, and the present and the past can talk to one another on equal terms. Modern Europeans are, in a sense, separated from their past by fundamental changes in their systems of values, as they have moved from a traditional towards a rational orientation, and as they have come to respect achieved success more than inherited privileges. Two hundred years ago the European theatre audiences laughed at Molière's *Bourgeois Gentilhomme;* now the *gentilhomme* is comic if he does not succeed in being a bourgeois too. But America has always valued achievement and deliberately rejected hereditary privilege.

In every society the things that actually happen are often far different from the things that are supposed to happen according to the accepted ideals, and this is true of America too. But myths are influential, and the mythology of America is concerned with individual effort, enterprise, adventure, a practical belief in equal respect for all people, equality of opportunity and, through the free exchange of goods, fair reward for each man's work.

The twentieth century has brought two big new elements into the foundations of American life. On the one hand, in a world made smaller by modern communications the United States has become a great power, unable to avoid involvement and responsibility in international affairs. On the other hand, at home the old system of individualistic free enterprise has had to be supplemented by massive state intervention. But the

Americans' view of themselves and their ideals have not been greatly affected by these changes. Their past, and the myths connected with it, have an immediate and continuing part to play in their present-day life. There is a continuous thread running back from modern industrialisation and automation, through the advance of civilisation along the old frontier, to the earliest beginnings of settlement from Europe.

It is very difficult to say just when colonisation began. The first hundred years after Christopher Columbus's journey of discovery in 1492 did not produce any settlement on the north American continent but rather some Spanish trading posts further south, a great interest in gold and adventure, and some colourful piracy in which the English had their part. John Cabot, originally from Genoa but a citizen of Venice, was established as a merchant in Bristol, England, when he made his journey in 1497; but his ship, the *Matthew,* with its crew of eighteen, did no more than see an island (probably off the New England coast) and return home. He and his son made further voyages across the north Atlantic which enabled the English crown to claim a 'legal' title to North America, but for a long time afterwards European interest in America was mainly confined to the Spanish activities further south.

The first beginnings of permanent settlement in North America were nearly a hundred years after Columbus's first voyage. The Englishman Sir Walter Raleigh claimed the whole of North America for England, calling it Virginia. In 1585 he sent a small group of people who landed in Roanoke Island (about the middle of the east coast of the present United States), but they stayed only for a year and then went back to England with another expedition, led by Drake, in 1587. A second group who landed in 1587 had all vanished when a further expedition arrived in 1590. The mystery of what happened to them has never been solved, but their unknown fate was not an encouragement to others.

The first enduring settlement in North America was in 1607. English capitalists founded two Virginia companies, a southern one based on London and a northern one based on Bristol. It was decided to give the name New England to the northern area. The first settlers in Virginia were little more than wage slaves to the company; all were men and the experiment was not very successful. Many died, and those who survived lived in miserable conditions. Two developments improved their situation: the beginning of the growing of tobacco, and the system by which the indentured servants of the company were enabled to become tenant farmers. By 1619 the colony had a thousand people.

Modern Americans are inclined to look back especially to the Pilgrim Fathers who sailed in the *Mayflower* in 1620, for a symbol of the origins of their new country. A group of Puritans from eastern England tried (after great troubles and persecution) to go to Holland in 1607 in search of religious freedom. Their first attempt to leave England was unsuccessful; they were arrested, and tourists still visit the prison cells in Boston, Lincolnshire, where they were kept. Eventually they did leave. After some years in Holland they decided to accept the help of some English merchants with a plan to move to America. They went back to England, and finally sailed from Plymouth in September 1620. There were thirty-six from the Leyden community, joined in England by sixty-six others, not all of them saintly. They had intended to go to Virginia, but when their ship reached Cape Cod, much further north, after a very hard voyage, they decided to stay in that part. They founded a town, which they named Plymouth, across the bay from Cape Cod, close to the place where later Boston was to grow. Because they started a new settlement they had to make their own arrangements for good order among themselves. So they made a solemn agreement together that their society was to make real the democratic ideals which had inspired them, as puritans, at home. Seventeenth-century England was full of speculation about the idea of the social contract; here was a real one to which, with the Declaration of Independence six generations later, modern Americans look back with reverence as an expression of their common purpose. The ideals have not always been followed up, but they remain as an important influence on American life.

The Pilgrim Fathers suffered terrible hardships at first, and half of them died during their first winter months; but those who survived for the first year managed to live on fish and reap a harvest from the land in the summer, with the help of friendly Indians. A year after they arrived another ship came from

England, and they celebrated this arrival, and the harvest they had gathered, with a feast of thanksgiving. The anniversary of their thanksgiving feast is still celebrated every November as a public holiday; Thanksgiving and Independence Day are the two great occasions by which Americans remember each year the two main stages in their national history, foundation and independence.

Between 1620 and 1640 the Pilgrim Fathers were followed by many more shiploads of settlers in New England. During the same period New Amsterdam was founded from Holland on the small island of Manhattan, further south. The Dutch administration was oligarchical, and the colony made rather slow progress. In 1664 (by which time there were 7,000 people in New Netherland) the English took over the colony and changed its name to New York. But Dutch names still survive, such as Harlem, originally a village a few kilometres up Manhattan Island.

Meanwhile, further south, Virginia developed and the settlers were helped by the beginnings of the cruel slave trade, through which merchants, mainly English, brought them slaves from Africa. And some small groups from other parts of Europe established themselves on parts of the middle coast.

The last of the main foundations came in 1682. At this time the Quakers had become the most energetic representatives in England of the Puritan tradition, and William Penn, a prominent English Quaker, led a group of religious sympathisers to settle in Pennsylvania, with attractive arrangements for the allocation of land and with a ready-made plan for a central town at Philadelphia. This settlement may be added to that of the Pilgrim Fathers at the centre of the American mythology; the Protestant individualism of these early pioneers has been idealised to provide the United States with a symbol of its original purpose.

The idealistic motives which inspired the first migrants to New England in 1620–40 still remain important for the Americans' picture of themselves. These early adventurers were for the most part intensely religious people, and though religion was not the only source of inspiration for their enterprise it was an important element in a set of motives in which one can see signs of consistency. Many wanted to escape from the oppressive religious and social atmosphere of the England which they left behind. Most of them were Protestants not ready to accept the structure of doctrine and religious practice of the Church of England which had been evolved from the Reformation. In England their beliefs caused them inconvenience and sometimes danger. But apart from that the England which they left behind was a society in which there was not very much scope for individuals to make their own way on their own terms by their own efforts. Their individualism was not only religious but also economic and social. European society had for a long time given each man a prescribed place. A European middle class, based on individual enterprise and effort, was already developing rather painfully, and more effectively in England and the Netherlands than in the rest of Europe. The idea of migration to America was attractive to some of the energetic individualists of the time, who were able to think for themselves and understand argument on political and religious and philosophical questions; they easily became critical of the pattern of English society. When they crossed to America they brought with them a combination of English attitudes and a criticism of those attitudes, leading to a determination to build a new society which was free of the bad elements of the old while preserving those which seemed to them good.

It does not take much imagination to think of the courage and other admirable qualities needed by the early settlers. They left behind them all security and everything that was familiar, they knew that they had a big chance of sinking in the ocean, they faced tremendous uncertainty and hardship in their new home. Each was far more of a pioneer than any of today's computer-aided astronauts.

The early American communities were religious, hardworking and serious. They were searching for a new freedom, but their enthusiasm for freedom did not prevent them from building their own demands for conformity, and they could themselves be intolerant towards unconventional people. Their enterprise and their ideals have provided modern America with an inspiration made the more lively by the fact that it is easy to concentrate on the favourable aspects of their story. But there are many unfavourable aspects too.

In the eighteenth century the settlements along the east coast were organised as thirteen colonies, each with a governor, under British rule. Relations with the home government were not always good. Meanwhile, the colonies grew and developed, their populations constantly reinforced from Europe and particularly from Britain, Holland and Germany. In fact, many of the settlers did not come willingly. Some bound themselves to serve for long periods to pay for their transport; some were convicts, transported in servitude instead of being hanged; many were thieves or murderers; others, people who had offended the English authorities in ways for which we would not have sympathy. And there was also the flood of Negro slaves brought over from Africa and sold to work in the plantations of the south.

Even the New England Puritans did some things which, by the standards of their own ideals, were thoroughly discreditable. For a time Massachusetts had a government in which religious enthusiasm was carried to tyrannical lengths, and in some of the provinces power was concentrated in the hands of a few privileged people. In their dealings with the Indians who were already scattered in their tribes all over North America, the colonists considered their own interests, and in the long run some Indians were assimilated with the new Americans from Europe, others relegated to a wretched life in areas designated as Indian reserves.

When the colonists won their independence they were still predominantly English in origin and in outlook, and for some time afterwards the English were still the most numerous among the new settlers. Later migrants of the nineteenth and twentieth centuries were for the most part not brought to America by ideals of the same kind as those which inspired the Pilgrim Fathers and the settlers who went with William Penn. The people from Ireland, Italy and Poland in particular, went to America in order to escape from intolerable poverty in their own home countries, and they were regarded as inferiors by the Americans of earlier generations. Even so, however different the position of the new arrivals as compared with the old, there is still a very important element in common among them all. All were in rebellion against something which they did not like in their own environments and all were prepared to take great risks and face great hardships in trying to build a new environment for themselves. All white American-born citizens today are descended from people who at some time made the great decision to move from Europe. This very fact gives all Americans a common cultural background, and all are very conscious of sharing it.

The picture of early America would not be complete without reference to the special type of development in the south, with a rural economy and organisation different from that of the northern states. The first settlements in Virginia were commercial ventures employing subordinate workers; English investors made money from the tobacco they planted. Later, further south, cotton plantations demanded labour on a large scale, and could most suitably be organised in large units. The need for labour was supplied by the traders in slaves brought over from Africa. So the population of European origin was supplemented by vast numbers of African slaves, who soon came to seem necessary to the economy of the south. Thus there is a certain irony about the inclusion of the south in the American story. The ideals of the Pilgrim Fathers and those who settled in the northern states were above all individualistic and egalitarian, based on the idea that all men were equal in the sight of God and that they should have equal consideration and opportunity in their earthly life. Yet in the south the plantations produced a social structure far more rigidly divided than that of the old England which the Pilgrim Fathers had rejected. From the beginning many Americans in the north found slavery offensive to their philosophy, while people in the south not only accepted slavery but seceded from the Union to preserve it. It took four years of war to bring them back and to free the slaves, but inequality survived.

Another unfavourable part of the story, concerning both south and north, is the relation of the settlers with the Indians. The people who crossed from Europe after 1600 landed on a continent already inhabited by hundreds of tribes of American Indians, and as the successive generations of settlers moved westwards they had to solve the problem of their relations with the Indians who were there before them.

The solution took various forms, including war, agreements and deceit. There was not a single Indian society, but many

societies, with different ways of life, some of them with highly
developed civilisations. In the long run the total effect of the
contacts between the Indians and the new arrivals produced
one main overall solution: the country became the country of
the European invaders, and little remains of the old Indian
civilisations except some ruins and some works of art—as well
as the names of places, including twenty-eight of the states.
There are still some Indian reservations, and some Indians live
in them, mostly in rather primitive conditions, and as something of a tourist attraction. They are maintained by an
economy which provides them with a standard of life which is
poor by normal American standards, but with some modern
aspects—it is difficult to live as a really primitive American
Indian if you have a television set. Other Indians have, with
varying degrees of success, become assimilated into the ordinary
American community as though they were themselves transatlantic migrants, and there has been some intermarriage.
The million or so Indians are a small proportion of the whole
population and not numerous enough to cause a problem on the
scale of the Negro problem, but it is not true to say that they
have been wiped out—indeed, after some recent population
increase, there may be more of them now than there were just
before immigration from Europe began. However, the number
killed during 200 years and the number still living in squalor
are great enough for the public conscience to be troubled.
There is dissatisfaction in the Reserves, and there are complaints of discrimination against Indians. Today's efforts to
remedy past wrongs cannot succeed quickly, and they face deep
resentments.

2. The Century of Massive Settlement: 1820–1920

When the United States became independent in 1783 the
settled part of the country consisted of a long string of farming
communities spread along the east coast, with a western frontier
undefined but steadily advancing into the continent. The
thirteen colonies of 1783 were organised units of government,
most of them rather large in area but very thinly populated

and, of course, with very difficult communications. The total population was about four million, much less than that of England at the time and indeed less than even that of Ireland.

Migration to America at this period was still very gradual, and the coming of independence did not lead immediately to a great new wave of people. Probably only about 150,000 people settled in America between independence and 1820, or 5,000 each year. The people already settled and completely identified with the country formed a big majority, so that the new arrivals felt themselves as a small number arriving in a settled community. There was thus every reason for them to assimilate quickly. In any case, by the fact of going to America they had shown their desire to incorporate themselves in this new community, and for the most part they came from England, sharing a language and in general sharing ideals and objectives with those who were there before them. In 1790 over four-fifths of the white population were said to be of English origin. Early American society was very English, in the sense that English ideas and ways of living had been taken to a new environment and adapted to it. Even as the new society developed its own characteristics there were many features in it which continued to show the English influence.

About 1820 the flow of new settlers from Europe began to increase dramatically, just at the time of the triumph of egalitarianism in the election of Andrew Jackson as President in 1828. Between 1820 and 1840 over a million people migrated to the United States, nearly ten times as many as in the previous twenty years, and many were from continental Europe.

1820 may have seemed a turning-point in the flow of migration, but 1840 could be regarded as another one. The development of steamships made the conditions of travel easier, though by any modern standards they were still terrible. The forty years, 1840–80, brought almost ten million migrants to America or a quarter of a million a year: fifty times as many as in the early years of the century. Many of the migrants during this period came from Germany, and for the rest of the nineteenth century German migration was no less important than that from England. There were also great numbers from Ireland, escaping from the poverty and famine of their own country, whose population actually fell rapidly during this period. The Germans,

mainly Protestants, were assimilated easily enough into the
English American society of the time, but the Irish kept themselves rather more separate. They did not need to learn an
entirely new language (though some were Irish-speaking), but
they were nearly all Catholics, full of resentment at the
domination of their own home country by the English, and
particularly by the English Protestant landlords. Around 1840
the absentee English landlords were extracting rent from the
Irish at a rate of about £1 per person per year, but one Irish
community of 9,000 people had ten beds between them, and four
families out of five had not even a chair or stool. Most Irish
households lived in unfurnished, windowless huts. In the famine
of the 1840s over a million died, but another million escaped to
England or America. And the new Irish Americans saved money
to help their brothers and their cousins to come and join them.
Irish immigrants met some hostile prejudice after a time. They
were supposed to be unreliable, and they certainly threatened the
Protestant domination. There were notices outside factories:
'No Irish need apply.'

For many of the migrants of this time the move involved not
only a change of homeland, but a change from farm to factory,
from country to town. American industry was developing
rapidly from the east coast to Chicago and beyond, and many
of the new migrants were absorbed in the factories that were
growing up everywhere. Evidently, they were not in a position
to press hard bargains regarding their conditions of employment, and nineteenth-century industrial development in the
American cities produced social problems little less evil than
those to be found in England and Germany at the same time.
But there was still a little more possibility of escape from the
bad conditions, and the great natural advantages in which
American industry developed made it possible for the real
wealth of the community to grow so that it soon outstripped
that of the old European countries.

By the middle of the century the United States had a larger
population than any single European country, and by 1880 it
reached fifty million. When we consider that ten million persons
had arrived as immigrants during the preceding forty years we
can see at once that the proportion of newly arrived people
to the whole population was very much higher by 1880 than it

had been in the early stages. The new arrivals up to the middle of the nineteenth century had found themselves a tiny minority in a community which was settled, in the sense that most of its members were descended from several generations of Americans. By 1880 there were large communities in which most of the people had been born in Europe. Many of the new arrivals were following friends and relatives who had come already; many had heard news of possibilities of employment. There were some compact national groups, particularly of Germans, so that some whole communities were composed mainly of people recently arrived from Germany. It might have been possible for large areas to have become homes for compact ethnic groups maintaining the German language and German customs, and so building up new little Germanies on the American continent, but in practice this never happened. Groups of Germans did keep their own national self-consciousness and they did live together, but they were always assimilated into the general pattern of American culture. Perhaps the Civil War (1861–65) had some influence in the development of the nation with its own full national self-consciousness, still absorbing the ever increasing numbers of migrants from foreign countries. There seems something of a paradox here; after all the object of the war was to settle the question whether the United States should remain one political unit or split into two. But the people newly arrived from Europe had nearly all settled in the north and could easily identify themselves with the northern position. To them the south was like a foreign country, and their share in operations of the war against the south made it possible for the northern Americans, who were after all the dominant section, to have a greater consciousness of being American.

   More than three-quarters of a million people crossed as settlers in 1882 and the flow continued, with some big fluctuations. New sources suddenly became important. For a time after 1880 the exodus from Scandinavia reached levels comparable with that from Ireland two generations before. One-tenth of the whole population of Sweden and Norway left for America in only ten years, 1881–90. The Swedes were escaping from poverty in a northern European country still dominated by aristocracy and still economically backward. Yet the very time of the great

Swedish migration was also the time of the beginning of
Swedish industrial development at home, which was soon to
gather momentum so as to bring Sweden in a short time to
a standard of living unequalled in Europe and approaching
that of the United States themselves. Like the Germans, the
Swedes who went to America in the last half of the nineteenth
century tended on the whole to move to the mid-west,
developing the areas west of Chicago. The German and Swedish
languages kept alive for a long time and are still spoken in
many communities, but this does not prevent this section of
America from exhibiting typically American characteristics.

After 1900 migration was stimulated and encouraged by the
activities of German and other shipping companies and by the
offers of cheap transport which they spread around areas of
European poverty. Twelve million immigrants came in 1900–
1914, one and a quarter million in 1907 alone. Two million
Italians came in ten years. A few only stayed long enough to
make enough money to enable them to return home and buy
some land in Italy, but most stayed in America and helped their
relations to come and join them. Although they were different
in language and religion, and even in appearance, their children
grew up as Americans and were quickly assimilated. Unlike the
Germans they were inclined to remain near the east coast and
particularly in New York and Boston along with the Irish in
those cities. Poles and Russians, many of them Jews, were added
to the Italians, and during the final years before the first world
war three-quarters of the new arrivals came from eastern
Europe and Italy. They were on the whole regarded as inferiors,
and they were conscious of having started late in the race for
wealth and prestige in the society they had come to join. It was
a very great advantage to be a white Anglo-Saxon Protestant,
and a disadvantage to be a Catholic or a Jew, or from Italy or
eastern Europe. These new groups had to practise a good deal
of self-help and community development on their own for the
sake of their own protection. Being different in so many
obvious ways from the established Americans they found it
hard to get themselves accepted.

By 1920 the total population of the United States was over
106 million (including ten million Negroes). Altogether thirty-
four million individuals had entered the United States as

immigrants since the beginning of settlement. Less than half of these had been from the British Isles, but as the flow from there had been continuous over so long a period America was still predominantly British in ethnic origin.

In 1920 massive immigration came to an end. Before then there had been laws preventing the immigration of criminals and other undesirable persons, but in 1921 restrictions were placed on immigration in general. The economic system of uncontrolled private enterprise was showing itself vulnerable to booms and slumps on a dangerous scale, and the prospect of a continuing flow of new arrivals on the same scale as before seemed frightening to American opinion. Also it seemed that, if there were no restrictions, most new arrivals were likely to be people ill-equipped for the demands of the new industry which, because of its technological advance, would not need an increasing supply of unskilled workers. The economic depression of the 1930s, with massive unemployment in America, almost stopped the flow, and in twenty years there were fewer new immigrants than in a similar period a hundred years before. Since 1950 there has been some increase, first slow then quicker, towards an annual rate of half a million.

The immigration laws of 1921 have been modified since, but the basic principle is still one of restriction. About ten million new immigrants have been admitted in the past fifty years, or about the same number as in the ten years 1904–14. The laws have aimed not only at restricting the total, but also at keeping the less-favoured nationalities out. The national quotas fixed in 1924 allowed the admission of up to 65,000 people from Britain and 25,000 from Germany, but no more than 5,600 from Italy. There was talk of maintaining a high quality of immigrants. There have been modifications in the quota system (allowing, for example, bigger numbers of Italians), but the laws had a racist flavour which caused much offence and a much more liberal new system came into force in 1968.

In fact there has been a change in the type of people entering America. Refugees from Nazi persecution included much of the intellectual cream of Germany and Austria, and the quota rules were relaxed for their benefit. More recently, a large proportion of the people crossing to America have been men with university degrees and high technical and professional qualifications, moving into good and well-paid jobs. Immigrants from England and Scotland are more welcome as a class than any others (except Canadians). They are the most easily assimilated because they speak the same language and are closer in culture than other Europeans, and they can, in general, more easily come over to take jobs with responsibility. Although the output of the American universities is so great, there is still room for British physicists, engineers and so on. If we look at it in another way, Britain has lately suffered severely from a 'brain drain', a steady emigration of highly-trained experts, well paid in England but able to earn much more prestige, as well as much more money, in America. Those of them who are scientists are attracted mainly by the more satisfactory conditions of work in America, better-equipped laboratories, more scope for their own professional work. Indeed the number of British doctors who went to America in one year recently was calculated to be equal to one-quarter of the output of all the British medical schools. In a way the American economy is being generously subsidised by the European countries which spend great resources in training men who then use their training for the benefit of America.

Some discouragement to well-qualified immigrants has been caused by the practice of American consulates which, before giving visas to intending travellers, have asked them objectionable questions about their political past. Anti-communism, particularly virulent early in the 1950s, led to a very illiberal questioning of intending immigrants at that time. A reaction against such methods set in about 1960, but there was some sign of a reappearance of a rigid attitude under the influence of the Vietnam war.

Since 1966 there has been a new discouragement to immigration. Any man who comes over to a regular job in the United States must come on a permanent entry-visa, and he may become liable to military service. And the same rules, essentially, apply to the sons of older Europeans who join the 'brain drain'.

As immigration has been at a fairly low level for fifty years, the proportion of wholly-American Americans is now steadily increasing. In 1910 one-seventh of the inhabitants had been born outside the United States, and one-fortieth in Germany alone. The proportion of foreign-born is much lower today, and seems likely to remain so. Perhaps the most useful device for identifying the people who have no real personal contact with non-American origin is by asking how many people had both parents born in America. Out of the United States population of 200 million, about three-quarters are white people with American-born parents. Many of these are aware of some European origin and rather fewer (a minority by now) maintain some sort of contact with family connections in Europe. Many have an ambition to visit the countries of their ancestors on holiday, and quite large numbers do so at least once in their lifetime, though in most cases only as a part of a visit to Europe. The attractions of Paris and London, the churches and art galleries of Italy, and the beaches of the Mediterranean, together with the idea of European culture and scenery in all its rich variety, are in general more interesting on their own merits to these American holiday-makers than the rather remote personal connection with a particular ancestral home—or even the cousins who still live there.

There are still a few communities, mostly quite small, which maintain a separate life within the American culture—and because the ordinary Americans are always looking for some variety in their homeland some of those surviving non-assimilated groups get much commercial advantage from being able to offer something different. The best example of this is the city of New Orleans, which keeps alive its French and Creole foundations. With the eighteenth-century iron lacework balconies of its Vieux Carré, its Mardi Gras carnival and its reputation for good food, it claims to be America's most interesting city—but in fact its distinctiveness is based on remote history, not on any continuing resistance to assimilation. The city is American in a special way, rather than French or Spanish. On a much smaller scale we may mention the Greek community at Tarpon Springs, Florida, which has much more recent origins and which attracts many tourists by its genuinely Greek atmosphere—the black-shawled women in its Orthodox church, the straight-backed chairs and the domino tables in its Mediterranean-style cafés. Above all, its Greek sponge-fishermen make a living not only by bringing in sponges but by letting ordinary Americans go on their boats. The houses and the cars of Tarpon Springs, the washing-machines and the refrigerators, may be all-American, but the Greek atmosphere is worth preserving.

In the United States as a whole there are now rather more than thirty million people with at least one parent born outside the United States or Canada. (The three million with a Canadian background can hardly be considered foreign.) The million Asians, mainly Chinese and Japanese, are evidently more difficult to assimilate, as are the three million immigrants from Central and South America (including the Puerto Ricans) and American culture has been rather unfriendly to these immigrants who are mostly fairly recent arrivals. During the war thousands of citizens of Japanese origin were interned, though no action was taken against Germans as a group, in spite of the fact that a minority of them showed sympathy with their country of origin in both world wars.

In the present situation, although there are plenty of elderly first-generation immigrants from Russia and eastern Europe living as American citizens, and a much larger number of younger people born in America of Russian or Polish or Czech parents, nobody expects these groups to provide a focus of sympathy for the contemporary communist regimes which are so much hated by Americans in general. On the contrary, of all Americans these people are the most implacably hostile to communism, and to the present governments of their own old homelands, and they are liable to organise hostile parades in the streets when Russian or eastern European leaders visit the United States.

No single part of Europe is predominant as a place of origin for first and second generation Americans; by language five countries or areas share most of the total: Slav-speaking eastern Europe with seven million; Germany, Austria-Hungary, Italy and the British Isles with around five million each; and Scandinavia with two-and-a-half million. The numbers may sound large in all, but most of these people have a rather hazy idea about their parents' foreign origins. Compact national groups are most evident among recent immigrants who have not yet found their way out into the American world. Such groups in eastern cities, particularly New York, are associated with poverty, misery, bad housing and social problems.

Two major European countries are only very slightly represented in the United States: Spain and France. The absence of
Spanish people is not surprising; the Spanish-speaking countries
of Central and South America have together nearly as many
people as the United States, and if we exclude undeveloped
Alaska the United States is smaller in area than Portuguese-
speaking Brazil. The early Spanish history of some coastal
settlements in the south of the United States, in Florida,
Louisiana and California, is kept alive by a few buildings and
by some names of towns, but by little else. France has been
represented by some famous personal contacts in American
history, but not many French people have emigrated to the
United States, either in the early days or in the great movement of 1850–1914. France has her own North American contact
in the Canadian province of Quebec, and Quebec, with its
French-speaking and Catholic culture, is the only substantial
part of North America to have stood out against assimilation
into the English-speaking world of the rest of the continent.
The most populous Canadian province, English-speaking
Ontario, is perhaps culturally nearer to the states of Michigan
and New York across the great Lakes and Niagara than to its
own Canadian neighbour Quebec. The United States has not
had any equivalent to Quebec in its own territory.

Although immigration has been fairly small for fifty years,
the population has recently grown much faster than ever before,
and even the rate of increase has been greater. This development is the result of prosperity. The Americans have surprised
themselves by the number of children that they have produced
in recent years. In ten years (1950 to 1960) the population rose
by over twenty-eight million, although there were only two-and-
a-half million immigrants, and reached 200 million in 1967.

American culture has developed from being a special branch
of British culture to become not only independent but also,
perhaps, the most influential element in the whole culture of
the west. However America is still English in ways which go
far beyond the language. Some English people who go to
America say with surprise 'It really does feel a foreign country.'
Others say, 'It feels very much less like a foreign country than
France does.' The second reaction comes nearer to expressing
the truth, though both are significant. Those English people

who say that to them America really feels foreign show by saying it that they were expecting that it would not feel foreign at all. The older parts of American cities, particularly near the east coast, look very like English towns, and even quite recently the influence of the admirable English design of the period around 1800 influenced much new building, in America as in England, though for really modern building the influence has been rather the other way around. The legal system is derived from the English system, and even now transatlantic precedents are cited in English and American courts of law.

Another British habit which has survived, rather surprisingly, is in the system of measurement (except for money). The Americans got rid of the English pounds, shillings and pence in 1787, when they took the word dollar from the old German 'thaler', and introduced a decimal currency. For measurements in general the metric system was made lawful by Congress in 1866, but in ordinary life distance is still measured in miles, yards, feet and inches, and weight in pounds and ounces.

All this does not mean that each modern British fashion crosses the Atlantic now, to be taken up by Americans as a lead worth following. American influence in modern Britain is stronger than that of Britain in America. There are specifically American usages in the English language, and most of them are widely known in England, whether they are words like *elevator* (English *lift*), or spelling like *color* and *thru* (a word which is not only spelled differently from *through* but also used as equivalent to the English *until*); but most English people know about these differences, and the variety merely illustrates the movement of ideas and habits between these two cultures.

An energetic cross-fertilisation across the Atlantic continues, and it covers industrial techniques as well as cultural attitudes. Industrial investment goes both ways, particularly from west to east, and managers stream across the Atlantic for production conferences. European students (particularly British) pour across the Atlantic to take higher degrees, and there is a massive interchange of university teachers. American jazz was taken up enthusiastically all over Europe many years ago, and now the British form of popular music, developed from it, excites Americans. The new culture of the younger generation straddles the Atlantic, its origins multi-national. But in all this, the Anglo-American link is kept especially vigorous by the absence of any linguistic barrier. The new ambition of parts of Europe for independence from America in political relations with the rest of the world was, in the late 1960s, reinforced by European misgivings about American action in Vietnam; but in the long run the cultural connection is far too strong to be destroyed by these political disagreements.

3. A People on the Move

After one migration the next comes more easily. New arrivals in America usually want to settle down to work and home as quickly as they can, but they may well move again sooner or later. American life has always had its element of change, of movement, some say of restlessness, and this is still so now. In some states only one house in five has people living in it who have been there for more than five years. In this story of constant movement we think at first of the early pioneers journeying westwards, taking a step further the adventure which had brought them or their parents across the Atlantic. Now there is movement, short and long, in every direction. Some leave their homes because changing economic conditions have put them out of work; others (more commonly now) go to better jobs, or move because they have been promoted. Even now some go without security and full of anxiety; but others, more fortunate, can move in comfort, with a good job and a new home ready waiting for them. Most college graduates, the new meritocracy, have studied away from home, and see movement as a condition and as one of the symbols of that success in life to which they almost automatically aspire.

Any person who moves to a new home (or who makes any other big change in his way of life) feels a mixture of elation and apprehension, and hopes to find something familiar to give him some security. For the transatlantic migrants from Europe this need has often been filled by family connections. After the pioneers from east Europe and Italy, many transatlantic migrants came to join brothers or cousins or village friends. But the modern movements within America are more often detached from consideration of the extended family. A man may have his wife and children to take with him, but if he changes his home for the sake of his career he is unlikely to be following his brother or cousin; more probably they are going off too, in the opposite direction. But the open friendliness of the suburbs, with their frequent departures and arrivals, gives a newcomer scope for feeling at home quickly, and many people belong to associations through which they can quickly find their way in the social life of a new community, to say nothing of the churches. But the less privileged, such as southern Negroes who go to the northern cities, have no such comfortable expectations, and in northern city slums they often find no link with others than the community of the insecure, with little to share but a common wretchedness.

People move in every direction, west, east, north and south, but certain trends predominate, particularly towards the west. There is also the movement of farm-people to the towns, as agriculture becomes more mechanised, though locally there is the flight from city centres to new suburbs as the town invades the country. Negroes move northwards in search of better opportunities (which they do not always find); retired people go to spend their last years in warmer climates; prosperous people move to better houses in better areas as their careers develop and their status improves.

The idea of moving is so thoroughly accepted that people tend to remain relatively unattached to the place where they happen to be at a particular time. At once we see a contradiction here. The United States is a system of separate states, and whichever state a person lives in is responsible for the whole of the ordinary business of government which affects him. It would thus seem that a man's membership of the state where he resides is a very important part of his political allegiance. Yet while a Frenchman may think it most unlikely that he will leave France to transfer himself to another part of Europe, an American living in Indiana most probably accepts the idea that it is quite likely that he will move to some other state during his lifetime. So although each state is a political unit having many of the characteristics of a nation state, a large part of its inhabitants at any time are people who have not always lived there. In some important ways America, for all its diversity, is also very homogeneous.

Movement within the United States has always been mainly

towards the west. In the early days there were always areas to the west of the fully settled parts of the country, and to these areas pioneers could go in order to make new homes in places which had never before been developed. Until about 1900 the idea of the Frontier was enormously important in the Americans' conception of their own position in the world. If a person was not satisfied with life where he was, he could go off as a pioneer to tame a new piece of land and make it his own. All through the first centuries of American development there was a steady movement of people and families who went to push the frontier of civilisation further into the continent. To some of these pioneering was a profession. They would spend a few years developing a piece of land, then sell it and move further west.

This process of movement is an important aspect of modern America's mythology. It can be idealised, but has its bad sides, all of which are too well known. Essentially the Wild West, which is the subject of a whole category of art particularly in the cinema, is the same thing as the Frontier. When a family moved off to begin developing some area on the western fringes of settlement, it had to face the problems of obtaining water and all the basic necessities of life, not to mention the possible hostility of Indians. A pioneer on the Frontier was always entirely responsible for his own affairs and survival, and there was nobody to help him. But as the movement towards the west became more intensive, so it was itself mixed up with the violent and competitive spirit of the pioneers. The worst dangers to a peaceful pioneer in the middle nineteenth century came perhaps not from natural conditions or from Indians, but from other pioneers. It was difficult to enforce law and order in such a large area with so little regular development, and some people moved to the west not in order to develop the country but to rob those who were doing the hard work. Even organisations which were engaged in essentially peaceful operations like railway building found themselves using violence in competition with rivals. The movement to the west has its heroes as well as its villains, and the dramatisation of this process still has an inexhaustible fascination—and not only for Americans.

By about 1900 people had occupied most of the land worth cultivating. There are still, even now, vast untouched spaces of desert and mountain, but when people develop these they work from well-established centres and depend on modern technology. There is no Frontier any more in the old sense. Now most of the movement of people within the United States is dictated by professional considerations. Workers of all sorts, and at all levels, are prepared to move in any direction to change jobs. Many Americans travel fifty kilometres or more to work each day, but others have to be ready to move altogether to find new jobs from time to time. More than a million families live in 'trailers', or caravans, houses on wheels, ready to move off to new places without having to find new houses or to disturb their possessions. These trailer homes are too big to be pulled by ordinary cars, and when they reach their fixed positions (for which they must pay rent) they are arranged like ordinary houses. In a way these trailer homes are symbolic of the Americans' relative lack of permanent attachment to particular places—and also of their ability to make themselves at home quickly in any new place, even though they do not expect to stay there long.

Of all the migrations of today it is the flow of people to Texas that comes nearest to the old myths of the west. Here the primary attraction is oil, though it seems that the rewards of enterprise have not been very evenly distributed. Texas is specially known for its oil millionaires, and there are plenty of them. But many who have not become millionaires have fared well enough, and this land of rugged individualism and violence under the burning sun brings in its own brand of fortune seekers. Texas will soon surpass Pennsylvania as the third state in the Union in terms of population, but its vast spaces (its area is a little more than that of France and England combined) are still thinly populated.

The most dramatic movement of all is into California. In 1900 this enormous state had only one-and-a-half million people. Now it has almost twenty million and is already the most populous state of the Union. It is difficult to see where the increase will end, unless it is stopped because there is not enough water. Up to now its momentum shows no sign of being interrupted. Hollywood (Los Angeles) was already the centre of the cinema industry by 1930, but in the thirty-five years since then the state has gained fourteen million new inhabitants.

The rate of movement into California during the 1960s (half a million people a year) is to be compared with the migration from Europe to the United States around 1900. But the people who come to California now do not come there as pioneers. They are not like the migrants from Europe, nor are they like the American pioneers who moved to the west in the nineteenth century. In general they move to California from a high standard of living in search of an even higher standard together with a pleasanter climate and more exciting natural surroundings than they can have in the East. California is exceedingly opulent. Its population has the highest proportion of people with advanced education at all levels, almost the highest income per person, the highest proportion of people living in their own homes in conditions which theoretically at least approximate to the modern American suburban ideal. This is the land in which there is not much to be seen that is old, and which most expresses America's view of itself.

The other western states of the empty lands to the east of California are drawing people in at an increasing rate. The total numbers who have gone to Nevada, Arizona and New Mexico are not yet impressive, and these areas still have few enough people to look like pioneering country; but the rate of increase of their population already exceeds that of California. Between 1950 and 1964 Arizona doubled from 750,000 people to 1,600,000, and its capital, Phoenix (Senator Goldwater's home) rose from 100,000 to 600,000—though its boom seems now to have overreached itself.

Within the well established industrial states of the east and near mid-west the centre of gravity has for long been moving westwards, to the areas of greater space. The New York–Chicago axis has been the basis of big industrial development for several generations, and the western end of it has many advantages. This movement is all in search of economic betterment; it is probably rather more attractive to live in the east than in Indiana, but there are many things which cause this centre of gravity of America, population-wise, to attract people from the east. Even so, other areas are still more attractive, and the industrial mid-west is not now gaining in relation to the United States as a whole.

One thing that leads people to move in affluent modern times is the desire for better climate, more attractive scenery, more agreeable living. Countless Americans working in Detroit or Indianapolis dream of retirement to Florida or California, where they will escape the cold winter of the north, and in northern cities the selling of plots of land for building new houses on reclaimed Florida swamps is quite a substantial industry. Some areas such as that round Tampa Bay in south-eastern Florida have specially adapted themselves as centres for retirement with all kinds of facilities for helping the elderly to move in comfortably and without anxiety and for keeping them happy in their new homes. This new world of the retired has added itself to the orange-growing, agriculture and forestry which have been intensively developed, but which have already brought in enough people for their needs.

But it is not only the old who like the thought of warmer climates. Many new industries which do not need to be close to their markets have been built up in the south and west, partly with the idea that well-qualified northern workers, already satisfied by their high living standard, will think that better surroundings and warmer winters will make their living standards still higher. So warm sunshine attracts both its flow of retired people, who come with a prospect of ten, twenty or thirty years' residence in their new homes, and its growth of industries which supply goods for other areas. Such new industries tend to need a high proportion of skilled workers, scientists and technologists; these create further demands for local industries and services, and for people to supply them. It is commonly believed that hot climates reduce people's energy and that the people of the old south walk and talk more slowly than the busy northerners. But now that air-conditioning is accepted as a normal provision in factories, offices and other places where people work, and that the mosquitoes and other dangers to health have been eliminated, the south is fit to receive modern industries and can help them prosper.

Practically every eastern state has an increase of population below the national level, and this indicates that when we take into account the natural increase there is a net loss of population through people leaving these areas for other parts. All the same, the position is complicated by the fact that a few of the north-eastern rural states which hitherto have not been highly developed are actually exceptions to the general rule in that their populations are increasing faster than the national rate. This is due to local movement out of towns, but does not imply a real return to the land. Most of the new country dwellers are townspeople who work in industry, commerce and administration, but want to live among birds and trees, and travel to their daily work. New Hampshire, for example, is a non-urban state mainly devoted to farming, north of the highly developed urban area of Boston. Its high rate of increase in population is due to people moving out of the intensively developed urban area of Massachusetts to live in rural surroundings, while remaining near enough to the town for work. Similarly New Jersey is increasing very rapidly, mostly with commuters from the New York area and partly with the spilling out of industry from urban New York into the country round about it. As more people live in one state and travel each day to work in another, the unrestricted movement across state boundaries becomes more obviously useful—though it creates new problems for the separate state governments.

CHAPTER THREE

The Forms of Government

The Capitol, Washington

1. General Principles

The whole story of the nature of political power in this vast nation of 200 million people is very complicated. The system has provided the rules for a society which has been stable enough to absorb the impact of the great waves of immigrants and of the development of the west. It has made it possible for the people to build up an immense and flourishing agriculture and industry. At the same time it has, on the whole, avoided oppression and provided the means of expressing reasonably well the wishes of this huge and varied population, so that violent grievances and discontents have been exceptional. Finally, it has provided the means for the United States to be a world power on a scale that has not been known before, using its power for influence, not conquest. There have been mistakes and tragedies, but judged by the standard of human history as a whole they have been rare, and overshadowed by successes.

Government and politics in America provide us with a vast and fascinating subject of study which illustrates the whole social and cultural life of the society. This chapter will begin with a very short description of the whole system, and then it will take some of the main aspects one by one and look at each in a little more detail.

The form of government is based on three main principles, federalism, the separation of powers and respect for the Constitution and the rule of law. Each American is subject to two governments, that of his state and that of the Union, and each has its own distinct function. The states have, under the Constitution, the primary functions of providing law and order, education, public health and most of the things which concern

day-to-day life. The Federal government at Washington is concerned with foreign affairs and with matters of general concern
to all the states, including commerce between the states. This
at any rate is how the system was planned at the beginning.
But for a long time the Federal government has been extending
its activities more and more. Many of the programmes of action
which a modern society demands need to be undertaken on a
nation-wide scale if they are to be effective. The Federal
government has in fact been active in the fields of social services, education, research of many kinds, and the ordinary
productive processes. Some of these developments have been
made possible by formal amendments to the original Constitution, but others have not. The words of the Constitution are so
imprecise that they have been interpreted in new ways, so that
some federal powers have grown within the system.

Soon after the Union was established, political parties
developed, and now two parties, Democrats and Republicans,
dominate the political scene. All elections must be looked at in
terms of party, and party influences the whole process of
government; but the two parties are very complex in their aims
and in their basis of popular support, though in the long run
they do, in their special ways, provide means of keeping
government close to the people.

At each level, in state and Union, there is a constitution
which defines and limits political power, and which provides
safeguards against tyranny and means for popular participation.
In each state, power is divided between three agencies, with
law-making power given to a legislature (usually of two houses,
elected for fixed terms), an executive (the governor), and finally
the judges of the State Supreme Court. Each state is divided
into counties, which have their own powers, and there are also
special-purpose areas for some functions of local interest.
Within the counties the towns have their own local governments, mainly as 'cities'. City government, with elected mayor,
council and judges, reproduces the state pattern on a smaller
scale. But each of the fifty states has its own peculiarities, and
one cannot attempt to describe particular systems one by one.
But one can say that all state and city governments provide
for election of legislatures and executives for fixed terms, and
all have devices for ensuring that each of the three elements of

government exercises a check on the other two.

The Federal government also has three elements — executive (the President), legislature (Congress) and judicial, and the three elements are checked and balanced by one another. The President is the effective head of the executive branch of government as well as head of state. He is elected for four years, and there is no provision for him to resign before the end of his term which, as provided for by the Twentieth Amendment to the Constitution (1933), runs for exactly four years beginning on 20 January following the election. No president has ever resigned, though several have died, and four (including Lincoln and John F. Kennedy) have been assassinated.

If a President dies he is automatically replaced, for the rest of the four year term, by the Vice-President, who has been elected along with him to be his potential substitute. In the words of the Constitution, he 'assumes the duties of the President', but he is formally sworn in as President. If a Vice-President succeeds to the presidency he does so only for the rest of the dead president's four year term, and during that time there is no Vice-President. Kennedy was assassinated in November, 1963, after two years and ten months as President, and his Vice-President, Lyndon Johnson, automatically took office as president for the fourteen months that remained of Kennedy's term. Then in November 1964, when the next presidential election was due according to the four year rule, Johnson was a candidate and was elected president in his own right, to serve for exactly four years from 20 January 1965.

The Vice-Presidency is a rather unsatisfactory office. If a President survives his four years (and of course most Presidents do) there is nothing particular for the Vice-President to do (except to sit as president of the Senate). Yet the accident of the President's death can thrust him unexpectedly into the highest office. Lately the Vice-President has generally taken quite a large part in the work of administration, and Nixon was a good example in 1953–61. Kennedy included his Vice-President Johnson in the highest policy-making meetings, and Johnson did the same for Vice-President Humphrey in 1965–68. All the same, it was possible for Eugene McCarthy to say of Humphrey in the summer of 1968: 'He said he won't neglect his duties as Vice-President while running for President. How a

Vice-President neglects his duties I just don't know.'

A President can serve for two terms consecutively, but no more. (This limit was introduced by constitutional amendment in 1951, six years after the death of Franklin Roosevelt, who had served three terms and then been elected for a fourth, which was cut short after four months by his death.) At the end of his first term a President is very well placed for being re-elected for a second, and many Presidents have served for two terms, or eight years.

The Congress is the law-making body. Like most parliaments it consists of two houses. The 'Upper' House (Senate) has equal representation for the states—two seats each—and the 'Lower' House is directly elected on the basis of more or less equal districts. This House of Representatives is elected at a general election held in November every second year (1966, 1968, 1970, etc.), and the newly elected House remains in existence for two years, with no possibility of being dissolved for a new election before the end of its fixed two year term. Each two year period is given a number in series from the beginning of the United States, so that the Congress produced by the election of November 1968, being in existence from 3 January 1969 to 3 January 1971, is called the Ninety-first Congress.

The House of Representatives has 435 members, and each state has a number of seats corresponding to its share of the total United States population. Every ten years, after each census, adjustments are made to take account of changes in population. States which have grown very fast lately, such as California and Florida, have gained seats recently at the expense of the states which have been growing slowly.[1] It takes about 400,000 inhabitants for each seat in the House of Representatives. After the 1960 census five states had one representative each, ten others had two each. The other thirty-five have three or more representatives each, and are divided into districts with one Representative for each district. In each district the election is by simple majority; the candidate who gets most votes wins the seat.

It is assumed that each district should have approximately

[1]Thus the 1960 census increased California representation from 30 to 38 seats, and reduced New York State's from 43 to 41. After 1970 California will have more seats than New York

the same number of voters, and as populations change this implies alteration of boundaries between districts from time to time. But the state authorities decide for themselves about the changes in the boundaries, and they may also keep a seat for election 'at large'. Until recently some states allowed districts to become very unequal and failed to change the boundaries, but the U.S. Supreme Court ruled that such inequality of electorates violated the Constitution.

The rules about fixed terms of office for President and Congress have prevented the type of instability that has been found at times in many European countries where the executive head of government resigns if defeated in the parliamentary assembly. They have also prevented the concentration of power that occurs in a parliamentary system based on two strongly disciplined parties such as that of Great Britain. But they have created conditions in which it may be difficult for any coherent policy at all to be followed, for example when the President is a Democrat faced by a Republican majority in one House of Congress—or even in both Houses. And the two major parties are so complex in themselves that a Democratic President may have difficulty even with Democratic majorities in Congress, just because he has not adequate means of exercising discipline among the members of his own party.

These, then, are the main outlines of the structure of government. We can now begin to look at the whole system in more detail.

2. State Constitutions

When the colonists gained their independence, one of their objectives was to give themselves a system of government in which each person would be able to live his own life without fear of being ill-treated or interfered with by political or religious authorities. Another objective was to be free of the damage and misery caused by war, and to ensure that there should be no room in their new country for the national rivalries and hatreds that they had left behind in Europe. The first objective they have pursued with remarkable success through all the changes of nearly 200 years, and with the second they had only one tragic failure until the changing scale of world affairs put an end to their isolation.

With the end of English colonial power the thirteen colonies became independent as separate sovereign states. They already had experience of collaboration against the English from the first continental Congress which they formed in 1774, and they had been assuming all along that independence would imply some overall formal organisation among themselves. The first task for each of the states was to establish a government which would provide people with assurance that they would enjoy the freedoms which were their main objective. The second task was to establish some kind of system of government over all of the states, so as to ensure that they would not make war against each other, and to give them means by which they could work together for their defence against any attack from outside.

For the first of these objectives each state made a constitution of its own and in its own way. For the second the states began by establishing a Confederation among themselves, with a Congress in which state representatives joined together in discussing common problems. But already there were many who wanted a more substantial organisation, and in 1787 a convention met at Philadelphia to draw up a constitution. The states gave up their rights to conduct separate relations with each other and with the outside world, but each state kept the basic powers of government for itself within its own territory. The United States Federal government should have only the powers which were necessary for providing for the matters which were of common interest to them all. They found their solution through federalism, and they made it work.

The early Americans had great faith in constitutions. They believed that if the powers of rulers were carefully defined and limited in legal terms they would not be used oppressively. America had produced little political philosophy of its own, but the influential men of that time were familiar with the discussion that had been going on in Europe on the nature of political rights and the type of government which would best correspond to belief in those rights. They were particularly concerned that government should be founded on the idea that each person had a fundamental right to be left to live his life in freedom and to enjoy the goods which he had obtained as a result of his own work or by inheritance. They recognised that government was necessary, and believed that for the protection of the citizens' rights power should be entrusted to particular people. But this brought a danger that those to whom powers were entrusted might abuse them. They were impressed by the argument of the French philosopher, Montesquieu, who claimed that the best safeguard against a tyrannical government was to be found in a division of powers. So the constitutions included definitions of the rights of people against the authorities, and political structures which shared out political power between legislative, executive and judicial authorities, and provided that these authorities should exercise checks against each other.

Every state constitution divided political power among three elements. The most important and fundamental power was that of making the laws. Each state provided for an assembly of persons elected by the people for this purpose. The right to vote was not given to women at this stage, and all of the states had restrictions of various kinds on the right to vote among men. In most states the parliamentary assembly consisted of two houses, of which the second or upper house was less democratic than the first and was intended to be a check on the possible excesses of the more popularly elected house. It was provided in every case that elections must be held at fixed intervals, so that an assembly once in power could not prolong its life without itself breaking the basic rules of the constitution.

Each state entrusted the executive power to a governor. In the time of British colonial rule each colony had had a governor appointed by the British king and under the orders of the British Government. The independent states kept the title of 'governor', which still survives today, but their governors were elected for fixed periods. They were never intended to be mere figureheads, and they have always exercised real powers, subject to carefully defined limits. Their duty is firstly to carry out the laws made by the legislative assembly, and secondly to do those things that are necessary for the conduct of government not necessarily based on specific legal powers.

Finally, each state had a system of courts, and the judges in the courts were not to be subject to the executive or the legislative authorities. This was to ensure that in any dispute the judges could act independently, even if the public authorities were themselves a party to the dispute. Here again the best parts of English practice provided the practical inspiration, while Locke and Montesquieu provided the theoretical.

Within each state there is a complete system of local government, with local authorities deriving their status and powers from the states. Local government systems differ from one state to another, but there are many similarities. There are some special features in New England states, but they will be ignored here. Each state is divided into counties (in Louisiana they are called 'parishes'), and on average there are about sixty counties to a state. As towns grow up they are given charters by state legislatures, defining the amount of urban self-government and establishing them as incorporated places, designated as 'cities', 'villages', 'towns', or 'boroughs'. The broad term 'municipalities' covers all of these designations, though the choice of the term 'city' or one of the others varies from one state to another. There are nearly 20,000 municipalities in the United States. All the largest ones are cities, though there are also many cities with less than 5,000 inhabitants—and some so-called villages with 50,000, particularly in fast-growing suburban areas.

As a city grows its suburbs tend to spread out beyond the city limits, so large numbers of suburb dwellers live in un-incorporated areas. There is normally some provision under state law for extending city boundaries, but it is not always easy to achieve such a change. A referendum among the people affected may well be required, and the suburban people may well be reluctant to join the city because they know that if they do they will have to pay more taxes. They may get better local services, but they will also have to contribute towards the city's rather high costs in dealing with many problems which do not affect the suburbs to the same extent. For some purposes, such as providing schools and drainage, special local units are set up, which may or may not correspond with ordinary local government areas.

The local government units have councils or commissions elected by the inhabitants, and in some cases the chiefs of particular services are elected too. The election of the mayor of a big city is a very important event, and the Mayor of New York holds an office generally regarded as more important than the governorship of a small state. All these elective offices have fixed terms, normally two, three or four years, though in most cases a second or even a third term is possible. Some cities have in recent years also appointed city managers on a non-political basis.

Municipalities and counties have their own sources of revenue, mainly in the form of a tax on property (though in some cases they may impose other taxes too). There is also in general a wide provision for the state to give grants to the local government units, and this implies some supervision. But the states do not appoint local officers of their own such as the prefects in France or their equivalents in some other countries.

All the thirty-seven states added to the Union since its foundation have constitutions based on the same principles as those of the original thirteen. State constitutions have been amended, but not so as to affect the basic principles. In all the states in the Union democracy is expressed through two main devices: firstly voting for persons to hold offices and to be members of legislatures, and secondly checks on the powers of those elected—coming partly from the separation of powers, partly from limits on the periods for which offices may be held. The Federal Constitution leaves it to each state to make arrangements for these elections, and in particular to make rules about the conditions under which people may be entitled to be registered to vote. The United States Constitution does not provide for universal suffrage, though it does forbid certain types of discrimination. Notably under the Fifteenth Amendment no person is to be debarred from voting because of his race or his colour. The Nineteenth Amendment forbids any disqualification based on sex, the Twenty-fourth forbids poll taxes with respect to federal elections. Each state can prescribe the minimum age for voting in all elections, as seems best to it. Most states have set the age at twenty-one years, though a few have a lower voting age: in Kentucky and Georgia the voting age is eighteen. Tests of literacy were for a long time given to people applying to be registered as voters, and sometimes abused, but now they survive only in a quarter of the states. No state allows a person to be registered as a voter until he has lived in the state for six months; half of the states require a year's residence, four (all in the south) require two years. Most insist on a minimum period of residence in the same county; in eight states the minimum is six months, in three states (all in the south) a year; in the others it is a shorter period, such as two or three months. The special question of Negro voting in the south is best discussed separately. At least, the principle of equal suffrage, as far as is practicable, is now widely accepted. But when we remember how important the ideal of equality has been since the earliest days of American settlement, we may be surprised that any restrictions exist now.

The states have been very ambitious in trying to make democracy real by giving the voters tremendous opportunities for voting. In each state the voters choose not only the members of the local, state and federal assemblies, but also the holders of the most important state and local executive offices. More than this—in recognition of the fact that elections tend to involve an effective choice between party candidates, the voters themselves participate in the choice of the candidates.

3. The Federal Constitution

Before going on to look at how government works in the United States we must look at the Constitution and the problems which this document creates. It has always been regarded with almost religious veneration, both because it is the main expression of the American ideal, and because of its success in translating that ideal into practice. It is a short document, and some of it is vague and uncertain in meaning. Also, it was written nearly 200 years ago, and the actual conditions and problems of an industrial nation of 200 million people are very different from those of the small pre-industrial society of the eighteenth century.

The First Article provides for the establishment of the legislative body, Congress, consisting of two Houses, and defines its powers. The second does the same for the executive, the President, and there is also provision in very general terms for a system of federal courts. The men of 1787 assumed that they were devising a constitution which would endure, but they also recognised that there might be a need for altering it, and they included provisions for amendment. The Fifth Article lays down the procedure for amendment, allowing either the

States or Congress to take the initiative. If the legislatures of two-thirds of the States demand it, Congress has to call a convention for proposing amendments—but this procedure has not been used. The other possible device, with Congress taking the initiative, is the one which has in fact been used: and this can now be regarded as the normal procedure. A proposal to make a change must first be approved by two-thirds majorities in both Houses of Congress and then ratified by three-quarters of the states—that is, now, by thirty-eight of the fifty states. The first ten amendments were made almost at once (1791); they form the 'Bill of Rights', and are really an extension of the original constitution. Two more amendments were adopted in the next seventy years, and the Thirteenth, Fourteenth and Fifteenth were passed only after the Civil War and as a result of the victory of the north. There have been ten more amendments since then, including one which outlawed alcoholic liquor in 1919 and one which allowed it again in 1933.

One clause which at first sight seems to be only a statement of what is obvious has been at the root of the difficulties of interpretation which are themselves a fascinating subject of study:

> This constitution, and the laws of the United States which shall be made in pursuance thereof . . . shall be the supreme law of the land; and the judges in every state shall be bound thereby, anything in the constitution or laws of the state to the contrary notwithstanding.

This means then that the Constitution of the United States takes precedence over all state constitutions and laws, and over laws made by the United States congress. But the Constitution also includes a list of the subjects concerning which Congress may make laws, and says that Congress has no other powers beyond those explicitly defined. The United States Congress does not have a general legislative power, but only power to make laws on these particular subjects.

Article One (Section Eight) of the Constitution gives the list of the topics about which the Congress has authority to make laws. They include defence and foreign affairs, citizenship and naturalisation (and therefore immigration) the regulation of commerce with foreign countries and among the states (but not within any state), and power to collect taxes to pay the debts and to provide for the common defence and general welfare of the United States. [1]

These are the main items on the list of powers granted to the Federal government, but the Constitution also includes statements limiting the powers of Congress. It provides, for example, that there shall be no *ex post facto* laws and that the privilege of the writ of habeas corpus shall not be suspended unless, in cases of rebellion or invasion, the public safety may require it. And above all the Bill of Rights, namely the first ten amendments, added to the constitution in 1791, places further limitations of a very general kind.

The most important of these amendments are the first, fifth and tenth. Under the tenth amendment 'the powers not delegated to the United States by the Constitution, nor prohibited by it to the states, are reserved to the states respectively, or to the people'. This statement is extremely important as it specifically lays down that any action by federal authorities which goes beyond the powers granted in the Constitution is unconstitutional, and must remain so unless the Constitution is amended so as to make it lawful.

The first amendment forbids Congress to make any law 'respecting an establishment of religion or prohibiting the free exercise thereof'. It also forbids any laws which might in any way take away freedom of speech or of the Press, or the right of the people to assemble peacefully and to petition the government for a redress of grievances. The fifth amendment provides that 'no person shall be deprived of life, liberty or property without due process of law; nor shall private property be taken for public use without just compensation'. These are some of the words that have made the problem of interpretation difficult and interesting.

[1] As the constitution was originally made, all duties, imposts and excises were to be uniform throughout the United States. At that time nobody had ever thought of imposing taxes on personal income. Later, when government began to become more complex, most governments in advanced societies began to put taxes on incomes, so that the rich could pay a larger amount than the poor, in proportion to their income; and later still, the rich paid not only more, but also larger proportions of their larger incomes. The terms of the constitution implied that as the taxes were to be uniform throughout the United States income tax could not be imposed at all by the federal authorities. And indeed when they did try to impose income tax, the courts found that such taxes were unconstitutional. Eventually the Constitution was itself amended in 1913, so as to allow the Congress to impose 'taxes on incomes from whatever source derived without apportionment amongst the states'.

The founders of the American Republic left behind them a Constitution which was the first of its kind in the world, and which has inspired dozens of other countries seeking political reform. In most other countries, during the past 200 years, one revolution has led to another, and constitutions have not endured. But the United States, which not so long ago seemed so new in comparison with the powers of Europe, now has the oldest written constitution in the world, and the longest period without revolutionary change except Great Britain, which in its turn has perhaps changed more profoundly in the matter of government.

4. Interpretation of the Constitution

The Constitution provided, in Article Three, that the judicial power of the United States should be vested in one Supreme Court and in such inferior courts as the Congress should establish. The federal courts were to have power to try all cases in law and equity arising under the federal constitution and laws. In 1803, a few years after the Constitution came into force, the Supreme Court established the principle that this required it to be the interpreter of the Constitution, with the particular function of reviewing laws (after they have been properly passed, but not before) to see whether they were in agreement with the Constitution. In reason, this conclusion was unavoidable. The effect is that, when a case arises under a federal law, and one of the parties argues that the law is itself contrary to the Constitution (which is the supreme law), the Court must decide whether or not the law is a proper exercise of power under the terms of the Constitution. If it reaches a negative conclusion, then the law is invalid and of no effect.

Evidently the judges of the Supreme Court have a very interesting power. We cannot say with certainty whether this development fits in with the original intentions of the founders of the Constitution; they had not really thought about the implications of the document which they had worked out. But the effect has been that in some ways the Supreme Court may be said to be almost a third house of the legislature. In several cases a law has been properly passed and brought into effect and then found to be invalid, so that all action which may have been taken under its terms has been illegal.

The Supreme Court is now composed of nine Justices. According to the Constitution they are appointed for life by the President with the consent of the Senate, and they cannot be removed except by a very special process on grounds of actual misconduct or incapacity.

If it were really possible to find judges who could interpret the meaning of the Constitution as absolutely infallible arbiters, by an ineluctable process of reasoning, everything would be satisfactory. But the chief points in the Constitution involve much uncertainty of interpretation. Just what does it mean when it says 'to control commerce between the states'? What is commerce? And what exactly is meant by 'between the states'? What about production? Suppose a factory makes goods, some of which are to be sold in a different state, is the actual production of those goods a part of inter-state commerce or not? And what exactly is meant by 'depriving a person of liberty or of property'? In so far as most laws forbid people to do things that they might wish to do every such law could be interpreted as an interference with liberty. Pressed to its most extreme conclusion this provision would seem to mean that no laws are to be made at all.

It would not be surprising to find judges interpreting these vague words in such a way as to suit their own concepts and ideas, and perhaps even their own political opinions. In fact we find that this is what they have sometimes seemed to do. So the President's power to appoint judges is obviously very important, particularly as there is no formal limit to his choice. Indeed, anybody with legal qualifications is eligible.

When one of the judges dies or resigns the President has to replace him by a new one, though he has to get the approval of the Senate for the appointment. It would, of course, be possible for a President to try to appoint a party politician completely sympathetic to his own political ideas, particularly as most American politicians are lawyers, and so have the minimum qualification to serve as judges. Presidents do in fact take care to appoint people who are at least in general sympathy with their own opinions, though the new judges are not usually politicians in the ordinary sense. But there have been times in which the members of the Court have greatly disagreed with one another about the way in which the Constitution should be interpreted, and many of the most difficult problems have been decided by majority votes of five against four or of six against three among the judges. At times it has been almost as though the Court simply consisted of two political parties, with one group of judges always on one side and the other group always on the other side. This is because the way one interprets such vague terms as 'liberty' depends very much on one's political opinions. At any one time the Court usually includes two or three judges who have held office for over fifteen years and others who are fairly new. Usually only a few have been appointed by the President currently in office. So it is not surprising if there is a mixture of political sympathies.

One difficulty arose from slavery. In the early days of the United States, right up to the Civil War, slavery existed on a large scale in the south. Seeing that the Constitution says that no person shall be deprived of his liberty without due process of law it would seem surprising that slavery could be allowed to exist. But very early on the Court decided that the Constitution merely meant 'the Federal authorities shall not deprive any person of his life, liberty or property'. This is because they recognised that the state governments existed first, and the principles in the Constitution were taken not to refer to those aspects of government in which the states remained sovereign. In the long run the people in the northern states became ashamed of the existence of slavery in part of their country, and the Civil War between the northern and southern states was fought in 1861–65. The southern states left the union altogether in support of their own rights, including the principle of slavery in their territories, and the war was immediately concerned with their attempt to leave the union. When the war was over, with the North victorious, the Thirteenth, Fourteenth and Fifteenth amendments to the Constitution were passed.

These provided that no state should deprive any person of life, liberty or property without due process of law and that no person should be deprived of citizenship or of voting rights because of his colour or because he had previously been a slave. So the passing of these amendments to the Constitution meant that it was now clearly the function of the Supreme

Court to ensure that all people, including Negroes, enjoyed the rights of citizenship. But the application of the principle has been very difficult, and new developments are taking place all the time, under the influence of the Supreme Court.

Sometimes the Supreme Court manages almost to add a new element to the Constitution by making new interpretations of the words of the Constitution in accordance with the ideas of the judges who happen to form a majority of the Court at a particular time. This is just as well. After all, the great words of the Constitution and its first fifteen amendments were all devised by people who had experience of a society completely different from the society of today.

For a long time, even laws of particular states regulating prices or conditions of work were regarded as improper interference with people's freedom to buy and sell on their own terms, though an exception was made for laws which were shown to be necessary for the public interest. The exceptions were difficult to define. In 1905 a state law setting maximum hours of work for bakers was found to be an improper interference with freedom, though state laws about the work of children and women were found to be permissible. And attempts by the Federal authorities to make rules regulating economic activity throughout the United States were found to be invalid unless they were obviously concerned with commerce between the states—and that term was interpreted very precisely. Anything that happened on a railway was a part of inter-state commerce, provided that the railway was used by some trains which crossed inter-state borders. But the Court considered that the production of goods was not part of commerce, so that federal laws could not regulate it; and they could not regulate commerce within any one state. So a federal law regulating conditions of work for children throughout the United States was invalid; it could not properly apply to factories which were engaged in production as distinct from commerce.

In the 1930s there were great difficulties. Franklin Roosevelt became President in 1933 on a programme of strong action by the Federal government to deal with the economic depression. His plans were approved by Congress, but were then challenged on the ground that they were unconstitutional because they involved the use of powers which the Federal government had no right to use. In several cases the Supreme Court found that laws passed as part of his programme were unconstitutional, and therefore void. But the judges in the Courts were not unanimous; some of the most important decisions were made by majorities of five to four. A few conservative judges, appointed before Roosevelt became President, were frustrating the policies which had been in his election platform. Then in 1937–39 some of the judges died or resigned, and Roosevelt replaced them by men sympathetic to his ideas. With its new majority the Court began to find new interpretations of the meaning of 'commerce', until eventually it seemed that all economic activity, including the process of production, was regarded as a single whole, and therefore able to be regulated by Federal rules as part of 'inter-state commerce'.

One line followed by judges in recent years has been to up-hold the decisions of the properly elected bodies, both federal and state, wherever there is uncertainty about the exact meaning of the words of the Constitution. This can justify them in upholding laws to regulate economic activity, but some have felt that, in order to be consistent, they must also uphold government action which may interfere with freedom in other ways, such as actions restricting the Communist Party. Judges who are liberal in politics have felt that they must uphold illiberal government actions if they are to be consistent. But in the last few years the liberal attitude has generally prevailed.

In the 1950s and 1960s the Court has begun to assume a rather 'positive' role. It has greatly extended its understanding of the rights of citizens, and particularly Negroes, to be treated without discrimination, and in 1962 it even ruled that the representation of the people in most of the states was unsatis-factory wherever the voting districts were very unequal in population. With these new interpretations the Constitution has come to be a much more effective protector of equal political rights, although it is no longer an obstacle in the way of regulation of the economy.

5. The Legal System

The legal system is complicated by the fact that there are two separate sets of courts with separate jurisdiction—state and federal. The United States Constitution left the states with full control over the maintenance of ordinary law and order within their boundaries, and jurisdiction over everything which it did not specifically give to the Union. Thus each state has its own laws, courts, police and prisons. Federal jurisdiction covers cases which arise under the federal constitution or under any federal law or treaty, and also cases which affect people outside the jurisdiction of a single state, for example controversies to which the Federal government is itself a party, or cases involving citizens or governments of different states.

In all courts, both state and federal, the basic system of law has been developed from the English, and this means that we must begin with Common Law. The principle of this is that when there is no statute law to define the rights of a case, the judge decides according to what seems to be right, but is guided by precedent—that is, by previous decisions of courts in analogous cases. Anglo-American Common Law has been likened to a wall, with bricks being added to it from time to time in the form of new decisions, each of which may create a precedent; but in this analogy the wall has notices stuck on it (representing the statutes). By now most of the wall is covered by notices, because statutes have been passed making definitions which provide for most of the controversies which may arise. Where there is no statute a court normally follows precedent, and any court is bound to follow the precedents set by decisions of higher courts. But the highest court is not fully bound to follow its own precedents, if it thinks that there is good reason for disregarding them. Such reasons are often connected with changes in circumstances, or in the currently accepted social values. Thus the United States Supreme Court ruled before 1900 that a state which provided separate public schools for Negroes was not giving them unequal treatment, and thus not depriving them of rights guaranteed by the Constitution. This decision created a precedent. But in 1954, looking at the situation again, the Supreme Court ruled that experience showed that after all separate education could not be equal in quality, and so by its nature did deprive the Negroes of equal treatment. A new precedent was established. Similarly, before 1962 the Supreme Court followed the doctrine that the arrangement of boundaries between voting districts was a matter for the state legislatures; so it could not interfere even when people complained that districts had unequal populations. But in 1962 the Court decided that equality of political rights, as guaranteed by the Constitution, required that voting districts should have as nearly as possible equal populations.

Although the English and American legal systems are completely separate, precedents still cross the Atlantic. When an English court is looking for a precedent to guide it, it may take decisions of American courts into account, and American courts may refer to English precedents.

A case involving the federal Constitution or federal laws, or otherwise falling into the category subject to federal jurisdiction, is heard first before a federal district judge; from his decision appeal may be made to the Circuit Court of Appeals, and possibly in the last resort to the Supreme Court. All the federal judges are appointed by the President and hold their offices with secure tenure, the principle of the separation of powers demanding that there should be no executive power to remove a judge.

Corresponding with the federal jurisdiction there is a federal police force, the Federal Bureau of Investigation, an agency under the President, who appoints its chief. There is also a separate federal prison system, and a criminal who has been sentenced for a federal crime goes to a federal prison.

The main points of interest in the legal system arise from the existence of the state and federal system side by side. In particular, it has sometimes happened that the state and local authorities have failed to take action against people in respect of some kinds of ordinary crimes. In the south, white people have committed crimes against Negroes without any action being taken against them, because those responsible for the local administration of justice have been afraid of getting themselves into trouble with the dominant white public opinion, or because they are themselves in sympathy with persons who do harm to Negroes rather than with the Negroes who have been the victims of unlawful acts. In some cases an act which is in the most obvious way a breach of state law may also, less obviously, happen to be against a federal law too, and there have been cases where southern criminals have been arrested

by federal police agents and tried in federal courts for incidental
federal offences involved in actions which in the first place
ought to have been dealt with in the state system.

All cases concerning ordinary crime, such as theft and
murder, and disputes between residents of the same state, come
within the jurisdiction of the state. States and local authorities
have their own police forces, which work closely together, and
the local forces may be regulated by the state.

Systems of courts and police differ from one state to another,
but there is a more or less general pattern. Small matters are
dealt with by justices of the peace or magistrates, and these
may involve moderate fines or short terms of imprisonment in a
local jail. County and municipal courts have a more important
jurisdiction. Above these are the state courts of original jurisdiction for serious cases, called district courts or superior
courts. At the highest level there are appeal courts which hear
appeals from the lower courts. In some states these are at two
levels, with a State Supreme Court over appeal courts at a lower
level. At all levels some judges are appointed to their offices,
some are publicly elected; states differ from one another in this
matter. In some cases the Chief Justice is elected and appoints
the other judges, possibly with the advice of a judicial council.
In some states the principle of recall operates with some of the
lower judges; a petition for the removal of a judge can be
prepared, and if it is strongly enough supported a new election
is held, which may confirm him in his office or replace him.

In both law and politics there have been scandals, corruption
and abuse of power. From time to time innocent people have
been made to suffer unjustly, unscrupulous people have used the
system to their own advantage. But the underlying purpose, in
states and union, has been to provide government based on
rational and humanitarian principles, and for all its deviations
the system has always tended in the long run to return to these
principles and to develop them. Freedom of speech implies
freedom to find out what is going on, freedom to expose injustice
and attack it. This freedom has never been seriously threatened.
Based on the Constitution it has helped to keep the governmental system true to the objectives of those who founded it.

EXTRACTS FROM THE CONSTITUTION OF THE UNITED STATES

Note: these extracts reproduce only the most important parts
of the principle sub-sections, and make changes in the
original order for the sake of clarity.

A. *Descriptive Section*

ARTICLE I

Section 1

All legislative powers herein granted shall be vested in a
Congress of the United States, which shall consist of a Senate
and House of Representatives.

Section 2

(1) The House of Representatives shall be composed of members chosen every second year by the people of the several States, and the electors in each State shall have the qualifications requisite for electors of the most numerous branch of the State legislature.

(3) Representatives . . . shall be apportioned among the several States which may be included within this Union, according to their respective numbers . . . Enumeration shall be made . . . every . . . ten . . . years.

Section 3

(1) The Senate of the United States shall be composed of two senators from each State . . . for six years.

(2) . . . one third may be chosen every second year.

Section 6

(2) No senator or representative shall, during the time for which he was elected, be appointed to any civil office under the authority of the United States.

Section 7

(1) All bills for raising revenue shall originate in the House of Representatives; but the Senate may propose or concur with amendments as on other bills.

(2) Every bill which shall have passed the House of Representatives and the Senate, shall, before it becomes a law, be presented to the President of the United States; if he approve he shall sign it, but if not, if approved by two thirds of that House, it shall become a law.

ARTICLE II

Section 1

(1) The executive power shall be vested in a President . . . He shall hold his office during the term of four years, and,

together with the Vice-President, chosen for the same
term, be elected, as follows:

(2)   Each State shall appoint . . . a number of electors, equal to
the whole number of senators and representatives to which
the State may be entitled in the Congress.

Section 2

(1)   The President shall be commander in chief of the army
and navy.

(2)   He shall have power, by and with the advice and consent
of the Senate, to make treaties, provided two thirds of the
senators present concur; he shall nominate, and by and
with the advice and consent of the Senate shall appoint
ambassadors, other public ministers . . . judges of the
Supreme Court, and all other officers . . . whose appointments are not herein otherwise provided for, and which
shall be established by law: but the Congress may by law
vest the appointment of such inferior officers, . . . in the
President alone.

Section 3

(1)   He shall from time to time give the Congress information
of the state of the Union, and recommend to their con-
consideration such measures as he shall judge necessary
and expedient.

ARTICLE III

Section 1

The judicial power of the United States shall be vested in one
Supreme Court, and in such inferior courts as the Congress
may from time to time ordain and establish.

Section 2

(1)   The Judicial power shall extend to all cases, in law and
equity, arising under this Constitution, the laws of the
United States, and treaties made . . . under their
authority.

B.   *Powers and Limits*

ARTICLE V

The Congress, whenever two thirds of both Houses shall deem
it necessary, shall propose amendments to this Constitution . . .
which . . . shall be valid . . . when ratified by the legislatures
of three fourths of the several States, or by conventions in
three fourths thereof.

ARTICLE VI

(2)   This Constitution, and the laws of the United States
which shall be made in pursuance thereof, . . . shall be the
supreme law of the land; and the Judges in every State
shall be bound thereby, anything in the Constitution or
laws of any State to the contrary notwithstanding. (Cf.
Marbury v. Madison (1803)).

ARTICLE I

Section 8

Enumerated powers of congress.

(1)   . . . to lay and collect taxes, . . . to pay the debts and
provide for the common defense and general welfare;

(3)   To regulate commerce with foreign nations and among
the several states;

(7)   To establish post offices and post roads;

(8)   To promote the progress of science and useful arts;

(11) To declare war;

(12) To raise and support armies and

(13) A navy.

Section 9

Limitations on Congress' powers.

(2)   The privilege of the writ of habeas corpus shall not be
suspended.

(3)   No bill of attainder or ex post facto law shall be passed.

10TH AMENDMENT (1791)

The powers not delegated to the United States by the
Constitution nor prohibited by it to the States, are reserved
to the States respectively, or to the people.

1ST AMENDMENT (1791)

Congress shall make no law respecting an establishment of
religion, or prohibiting the free exercise thereof; or abridging
the freedom of speech, or of the press; or the right of the
people peaceably to assemble, and to petition the government
for a redress of grievances.

5TH AMENDMENT (1791)

No person shall be . . . deprived of life, liberty, or property,
without due process of law; nor shall private property be taken
for public use without just compensation.

13TH AMENDMENT (1865)

Section 1

Neither slavery nor involuntary servitude . . . shall exist
within the United States.

14TH AMENDMENT (1868)

(1) All persons born or naturalised in the United States . . .
     are citizens of the United States and of the State wherein
     they reside. No State shall make or enforce any law which
     shall abridge the privileges or immunities of citizens of
     the United States; nor shall any State deprive any persons
     of life, liberty, or property, without due process of law;
     nor deny to any person within its jurisdiction the equal
     protection of the laws.

15TH AMENDMENT (1870)

Section 1

The right of citizens of the United States to vote shall not be
denied or abridged by the United States or by any State on
account of race, color, or previous condition of servitude.

CHAPTER FOUR

Parties and Elections

Electioneering: President Nixon in 1968

1. The Parties

Party politics and elections in America seem in a way to be simple, because there are only two parties; yet they are also very complicated. Neither of the parties has any definite single permanent approach to the problems of government. It would be quite reasonable to say that the Democratic Party is the party of the left and the Republicans the party of the right, but this is only partly true. What we can say is that in most of the northern part of the United States a rather high proportion of people who are relatively rich vote for Republican candidates, and a rather high proportion who are relatively poor vote for Democratic candidates. The Democrats also tend to attract votes from people who feel conscious of belonging to 'outside' groups: Italians, Irish, Negroes, Catholics, Jews, and also intellectuals. There are also more people belonging to such groups among Democrat than among Republican office-holders. So on the basis of popular support one can say that in most of the country the parties to this extent look like left and right. On the other hand in the southern states until very recently practically everybody voted for Democratic candidates for all offices except that of President, and in practice within each of the southern states the Democrats have been almost the only party. And in most of the southern states the Democrats are much further to the right than most of the Republicans are in the north. So if we look at the Democratic Party as a whole it is hardly fair to say that it is just a party of the left. Lately the Republicans have been gaining votes in the south, mainly on the argument that southern rightists should vote for a right wing party. The old Democratic domination may soon fade away.

In the last few years certain principles have emerged. For forty years up to 1968 all Republican candidates for the presidency were to the right of their Democratic rivals. In the 1964 presidential election it was quite clear that the Republican candidate, Barry Goldwater, was a man of the extreme right, whereas the Democratic candidate, Lyndon Johnson, was a man of the left and centre. But Goldwater was much too far to the right for many Republicans. The party had chosen him, but many Republicans disapproved of the choice. When the election was held in November the Democrat, Johnson, won by a huge majority, because many people who usually voted Republican were prepared to vote against an extreme right wing Republican and for a moderate Democrat. At the same time, Goldwater got a majority of votes in the most extremely conservative southern states, where people who were normally supporters of the Democratic Party voted for the Republican candidate because they agreed with his policies more than with those of the Democratic candidate Johnson. In 1968 Nixon won as a Republican partly because he appeared to be a moderate candidate, with policies not very obviously different from those of his Democratic rival. The extreme conservatives in the south found both of the main candidates too moderate, and voted for their own candidate, Wallace, but his support was not important enough outside a few southern states.

Now we have yet another complication. In one or two states, notably New York, the Republicans are apparently trying to appear further to the left (by European notions) than the Democrats. Each party is liable in different places to adopt a line of approach which seems to be inconsistent with the policy of the same party in another place, or even with the policy of the same party in the same place at another time. The differences between one party's policy in one time and place and the same party's policy at another time and place may be due to the inclinations of the people who happen to have gained control over the party machine for a time, or they may be due to calculations about the best way of winning votes. When Lyndon Johnson was first elected to federal office as a Representative from Texas, he was more conservative than he later showed himself when he was leader of the Senate and when there seemed to be a chance that the Democrats might choose him as presidential candidate. Richard Nixon too began his political career as a man of the right, but long before 1968 he had built up a new reputation for being moderate.

In order to understand the nature of American party politics we must begin by recognising that very many offices are filled by public election. When an American voter votes in November in the presidential election each leap year, he is at the same time voting in several other elections as well. He is also voting for a person to serve in the United States House of Representatives as the member for the particular district in which he lives. As his state has two members of the United States Senate, each elected separately for a six year term, the voter has a vote for a senator in two elections out of three. He is probably voting in addition for at least one member of his state legislative assembly and perhaps for a member of his state senate. At regular intervals he votes to choose the governor of his state, the mayor of his town or city and the holders of several local public offices at the level of the state and of the county or local community. These may include controllers of local commerce, directors of education, and the holders of many other local administrative offices. Every second year, in November, then, there is voting at the same election to fill many offices, local, state and national, and every fourth year the election is for the Presidency as well as all these other positions. At any of these elections the voters may be asked in addition to decide for or against one or more local proposals submitted to a referendum, though referendums may be held at other times too.

With so many jobs to be filled by election it would be very inconvenient if there was a separate election for each position. So it is convenient that most of the elections are held together in November, so that a voter needs to make one visit to the voting place to record his vote for many different offices at the same time and in the same operation. Some states still use ballot papers for voting, others have mechanical devices so that the voter pulls a lever to record his vote. In either case the voting is, of course, secret. The operation is simplified by the fact that the serious candidates for the national and state offices stand as Republicans or Democrats, and it is often possible to vote a 'straight ticket', supporting all the Democratic (or Republican) candidates for the different offices. (We must say

'often possible', because some local candidates are non-party.)
But, as we shall see, the voter has already had a part to play
in deciding who the main party candidates are to be. And even
when a straight ticket vote is possible, many voters will prefer
to mix their votes, choosing perhaps a Republican for senator
and a Democrat for governor. Personality, as well as particular
local issues, may lead a voter to mix his preferences at a single
election.

2. Choosing the Candidates

The most remarkable device of American politics is that of the
so-called primary election. The party candidates for different
offices (except the Presidency) are everywhere chosen by some
sort of open election within the party. That is to say, in order
to become the Democratic candidate for a particular office, a
person must have been chosen (usually against rivals) at an
election in which at least all local members of the Democratic
party may take part. The rules about participation in the
primary elections are not the same in all states, but they are now
regarded not just as private activities of the parties (as in most
of Europe) but as an essential part of the public election process.
The arrangements for the primary elections are made by the
public authorities and they are controlled by state laws.

The main difference between types of primary election is that
between 'open' and 'closed' primaries. Most primary elections
are closed. This means that although both parties may hold
their primary elections at the same time and in the same place,
a voter who wants to vote in the primary election must first
register formally as a member of one party; when a primary is
closed, people are not allowed to be members of both parties for
the purpose of voting. However, a person who is registered as,
say, a Democrat is still perfectly free to vote for Republican
candidates at the final election when he has to choose between
party candidates. In some states anybody may vote in the
primary election of either party, without having to declare his
party membership. In these the primary is called 'open'. The
whole system is intended to ensure a really popular decision in
choosing candidates, so that the business of choosing party
candidates does not become controlled by a few people (or even

by one person) who have gained positions of special power and
influence inside the party. Obviously the system has not
achieved perfect popular control, but it has reduced the power
of corrupt local party bosses, who in the past became controllers of local party machines, and ensured that their
supporters were chosen as candidates.

3. Election of the President

The election which is most publicised outside America and
which excites greatest interest inside America is the election
of the President. The President is elected for four years, and
it is possible, and now fairly usual, for the President at the
end of his four years to be elected for a second term of office.

The President is elected by all the people, but the Constitution
originally provided that he was to be indirectly elected by an
electoral college whom the people were to choose, each state
voting separately. That system was still in force in 1968.
Technically the election of President is in two stages: first, the
process by which the people in each state choose the list of
presidential electors for the state, and secondly, the process by
which the electors from all the states cast their votes for
presidential candidates. It should be made clear that this first
stage, at which the people are choosing the electors, is not a
primary election and should not be confused with primary
elections. The rule is that each state has a number of
presidential electors which is the same as the total number of
members of the House of Representatives for that state plus
two, the two being equivalent to the number of senators for
the state. The number of members of the House of Representatives from a state depends on the population, and each state has
two senators. So the small states, being heavily over-represented
in the Senate, are somewhat over-represented in the electoral
college. For example, in 1960–70 the state of New York had
forty-one members of the House of Representatives and two
members of the United States Senate, and so it had forty-three
presidential electors, or, in other words, forty-three electoral
college votes. The state of Wyoming had one member of the
House of Representatives and two senators, so it had three
electoral college votes; yet New York State has forty times as

many inhabitants as Wyoming. As the total number of the House of Representatives is 435, and as the Senate has 100 members, there are altogether 535 presidential electors, including three for the District of Columbia, which has no seats in Congress.

The original idea was that the people of a state should choose the presidential electors, and that then all of the electors together should choose a president. But a very long time ago it became the practice that the presidential electors acted as mere party nominees. When the voters of a state choose presidential electors, they have to choose between a Democratic list and a Republican list, though there may also be other lists put up by other parties, such as Socialists and Prohibitionists. (These long-surviving minor parties have until now been ineffective, but some splinter parties, broken off from the Democrats or Republicans, have been important in a few elections.) Late in the summer before an election every fourth year, each of the two main parties has already chosen its candidate. This means that the list of electors for the Democrats are already committed to voting for the Democratic candidate. And so, if a voter votes for the Democratic list of electors he is effectively voting for the official Democratic candidate for the presidency; the election is really direct within each state. The Constitution's provision for indirect election now means nothing at all in reality. This is so much recognised that the voting papers (or machines) regularly put the name of the Democratic candidate (in 1968 Humphrey) and Republican candidate (in 1968 Nixon) before the voters so that they are hardly aware that they are choosing a list of electors at all.

On the other hand, this rationalisation of the two stage process does not mean that all the Americans simply vote in one single block so as to choose a President by a majority. In each state the electors chosen are those who comprise the list of the party that gets most votes in that state. Supposing that in New York state 5,000,000 people vote for the Democratic list (i.e. the Democratic candidate) and 4,900,000 for the Republican list, then all the forty-three electoral college votes for New York State go to the Democratic candidate, and none to the Republican. This is, of course, an absurd arrangement, and it

A party convention   *New York mayoral election: the writer,
Norman Mailer, a candidate in 1969,
attends a political rally*

could possibly lead to a person being elected President just because he had obtained the right number of presidential votes although he had won fewer popular votes than his main rival. This has indeed happened twice, but not since 1900. But when there is a third candidate with serious support the result may look very strange, as in the election of 1912 when Theodore Roosevelt was a so-called progressive candidate and split the Republican vote. Wilson, the Democrats' candidate, won under forty-five per cent of the popular vote but won the election with a huge majority in the electoral college: 435 against 88 for Roosevelt and only 8 for the official Republican, Taft—though the last two between them shared more than half of the popular vote.

There have been cases in which some states have refused to go along with the majority of their own party. In 1948 the Democratic party in some southern states refused to support Truman, and put up their own candidate (Thurmond), against both the candidates of the major parties. He received less than three per cent of the popular vote but did fairly well in terms of electoral college votes (39 out of the 531) because his support was concentrated, and he won in some states. But a fourth candidate, a leftist breakaway from the Democrats, who received nearly the same popular vote, won no electoral college votes because his support was scattered. Truman won, to the surprise of nearly everyone, even without the support of these southern states. The candidature of George Wallace in 1968 looked like a repeat performance of Thurmond's. Although Wallace called himself an Alabama Democrat he did also campaign all through the west and mid west preaching both states' rights and firm action to maintain 'law and order', and he had some success in a few of the northern states, mainly from white people with anti-Negro prejudices.

Partly because the two major parties have so many internal differences, the personality of a presidential candidate is very important. In 1952 Eisenhower won the Republican nomination and then the Presidency mainly because of his great personal popularity and fame as a general; two years earlier he had not been identified with either party. Millions of people who in general regarded themselves as Democrats voted for Eisenhower as a man rather than as a party leader—and many of them

voted for Democratic candidates for Congress, and for state and
local offices, at the same time as they voted for him, as a
Republican, in the presidential election. John Kennedy owed
his success in 1960 to his personal appeal, and in 1968 Hubert
Humphrey was defeated partly because he had been overshadowed for four years by Lyndon Johnson. Humphrey as
Vice-President had not been able to build himself up as a
distinctive and independent politician. Although the presidential
election is fought between party candidates, it is also very
much a personal contest.

When a big electorate has to choose a man for a high office,
and there is real competition, there must be devices for choosing
the candidates who will oppose one another, and these devices
can always be criticized for being undemocratic. In the choice of
the party candidates for the Presidency the politicians usually
have the last word, but the people play a bigger part than in
parallel processes in most other countries. The whole confused
and untidy six-month pageant expresses much of the American
character.

As we have seen, the last stage is the formal act of the
electors who merely confirm the choices between Republican
and Democratic candidates which the people have made at the
effective election in November. Before this comes the process
by which the two main parties choose their candidates. Each
party does this at a convention held during the summer. The
convention is a gathering of important personalities representing the state party organisations. The six months before the
convention are occupied in preparation for it.

In most European countries, some members of parliament
become leading politicians and thus claim support as party
leaders and possibly prime ministers. But in America, because
neither of the main parties has any effective national organisation, there is no real national party leader except for the
President actually in office. He is indeed a real leader of his
party, and this is one reason why he is likely to be chosen by
his party a second time when he is coming to the end of the four
years for which he has been elected. The party that does not
have the presidency, on the other hand, often has no identifiable
leader except during the three months between its convention
and the election.

The convention of each main party, held in the summer before
a November election, is then a gathering of representatives of
the state party organisations, and its only real purpose is to
choose the party's candidate for the office of President. It does
also have the task of formulating party policy, but this statement of policy is usually a series of rather meaningless phrases.
Although the presidential convention, taking place once every
four years, is the only occasion on which a party has a general
meeting, the business of making party policy forms only a very
small part of its task. Thus we can say that it is very difficult
ever to define the policy of either party. This is partly because
each of the parties is such a confused organisation, and there
is always plenty of disagreement between the people who have
control in one state and those who have control in another
state. The statement of policy has to be a compromise satisfying
many different opinions, but at the end of it all there is always
one man as the party's candidate.

During the six months or more before the party convention
the various people who have some hope of being chosen run
their own campaigns inside their own party. A special point of
interest here is that although the party has large funds, which
are used by the party to help its official candidate at the regular
election in November, the individuals who hope to be chosen
as party candidate have to build up their own funds, either
from their own personal wealth or from contributions made in
a short time by people sympathetic to them as individuals.
These funds have to be collected rather quickly, during the few
months before the convention. Running a personal campaign
to try to win a party nomination is very expensive, particularly
as it is useful to be able to buy time on television networks for
a candidate to get himself known.

When the party convention meets it may have a real choice
to make. In some cases it is pretty clear before the meeting
starts who will be chosen. In 1964 Johnson had no serious
rivals for the Democratic nomination, as he was already
President after the death of Kennedy. But in other cases (as
in 1968 in both parties) there is a real struggle, and it is very
uncertain which candidate will win the nomination. There are
sometimes two serious contenders, sometimes several. And
there are always a few others who enter the race without

having any chance of being chosen.

Each party allows each state to send a number of delegates determined according to the party's own rules, and based on the population; a state may get additional delegates according to the number of votes cast in the state for the party at the previous election. The Republican Convention in 1968 had 1,333 delegates, the Democratic had 3,099, but some delegates had only half a vote each, and the total number of votes counted was 2,622.

At first it takes some time to ensure that the members of the state delegations have proper credentials, and to prepare that empty policy-statement, the party platform. Meanwhile the candidates stay in their headquarters in nearby hotels, and the serious bargaining begins.

Then the convention moves towards the choice of its candidate. First the names of the states are called out in alphabetical order, beginning with Alabama. When the name of a state is called the spokesman of its delegation may make a speech nominating a candidate—or he may say nothing for the time being. The honour of nominating a major candidate is usually left to the delegation of his own state, or a state with which he has some connection. A spokesman may well propose a 'favourite son', that is a person from the state who seems to have no chance of being chosen. At the Republican Convention of August 1968, at Miami Beach, twelve people were nominated, most of them state governors. But only three of these, Nixon, Rockefeller (Governor of New York) and Reagan (Governor of California), were serious candidates.

When a name is proposed by a speaker on behalf of a state delegation, those in favour cheer, and the amount of support for him in the whole convention is indicated to some extent by the amount of noise that is made and by how long the noise lasts. The loud demonstration is part of the ritual developed more than a hundred years ago. By the 1920s, with the help of mechanical devices, the noise in support of a serious candidate was beyond human endurance; the racket could last for an hour. But recently this crude assessment has been of little importance. The length of each demonstration is limited by the rules, and has mainly a ritual significance.

After the nominations have been made, each state delegation

announces in turn how it is voting; either all its votes for one candidate, or splitting the vote among two or more—e.g. twenty-five for Nixon, four for Reagan.

Some of the state delegations have arrived at the convention clearly decided to back one candidate, some to back another candidate, and some are divided or undecided. The delegations from the states which have held presidential primary elections will at first act according to the voting in the primary elections, but are not finally bound by them. And there may be some delegations who wish in the first place to support a candidate with no apparent chance of winning, but who have already decided to switch to one of the strongest two or three candidates if it becomes obvious that their first choice has no chance at all. This means that before the formal process of calling out the name of the states, the state delegations have spent a good deal of time in private discussions and bargaining together. Probably the effect of these bargainings and the organisation connected with them has become more important in recent times, as the organisation of personal campaigns has become more effective. Senator Goldwater had been working for four years to try to ensure his nomination before the convention chose him as Republican candidate in July 1964. His success was due, more than anything else, to the effectiveness of the organisation that had been developed by himself and his immediate supporters. The same could be said about John F. Kennedy in securing the Democratic nomination at the convention of July 1960. The final choice is not made until one candidate has received the votes of more than half of the delegates. If nobody gets this absolute majority on the first ballot, a second ballot is held, then a third, and so on until there is an overall majority for somebody. Once the Republicans had to hold thirty-five ballots, but recently a first ballot victory has been more usual, and both Nixon and Humphrey were chosen on first ballot in 1968.

The way in which the state party machines decide which of the possible candidates they would like to support in the struggle for the party nomination varies from one state to another. In two-thirds of the states the people who have obtained influence in the state party organisation make a preliminary decision, and so advise the party delegates before it goes to the national convention as to which of the candidates

they should support. This process is often very complicated.
Quite small but determined groups may sometimes be quite
influential. One important factor may be that few people come
to preliminary meetings in precincts. This lack of readiness
among ordinary people to take trouble may help the established
party leaders, but it may also, sometimes, be useful to energetic
groups who are opposed to the main leadership.

In one-third of the states there is a kind of presidential
primary election. That is to say, each of the parties organises
a special primary election at which the registered party members are able to say which of the possible presidential
candidates they like best. These primary elections are not all
held at the same time but are spread out through the period
from March to June. Usually the small state of New Hampshire,
in New England, holds its presidential primaries first, and the
result of this gives some indication as to which of the possible
candidates is likely to be the most favoured. Then the other
states which have primary elections follow one by one. The
people who have some hope of being nominated as the party
candidate do not necessarily all take part in all these state
primaries. In fact it sometimes happens that none of the main
candidates is a candidate at some particular state primary. So
the results of these primary elections are really very confused.
A declared candidate in a primary in one of these states has to
run a large campaign against his rivals, and this costs a good
deal of money. It is therefore necessary to have large funds,
though these may be contributed by personal supporters. If the
funds are too small, then a candidate is liable to be in trouble.
It is well known that Hubert Humphrey dropped out of the
contest for the Democratic nomination in 1960 when his funds
were exhausted; but in 1968 Eugene McCarthy's supporters,
well aware of the importance of money and believing that he
had a real chance, helped to make his candidature a serious
one by massive contributions.

In some of the states which have presidential primaries the
voters are allowed to write on the ballot paper the name of a
person who is not a candidate in that particular election. So it
is possible for someone to be a half-candidate, by not having
his name put forward officially, but hoping that many people
like him so much better than any of the declared candidates

that they will not vote for any of those, but write his name on
the ballot paper and vote for him. It has been known for a
person to get more votes, even without being a candidate,
than any of the people who are candidates. Supporters of a
man who is not a declared candidate may run a campaign on
his behalf to get write-in votes for him.

The rules in the different states which have presidential
primaries vary, and each of these contests is carried on quite
separately from the others. Even when a state party has chosen
someone by a majority of its registered members, the state
delegation is only obliged for a short time to support that
candidate when it reaches the convention. If soon after the
convention has started it becomes evident that a candidate
chosen through a state primary has no chance of winning, then
the state delegation may transfer its support to another of the
candidates. A candidate may concentrate on those states which
have primary elections, in the hope of showing that he can win
popular support, or he may work mainly through the party
machines; he may do both. In 1968 Humphrey and Nixon concentrated on the machines in the Democratic and Republican
Parties respectively, while McCarthy (and Robert Kennedy,
before he was murdered) and Rockefeller concentrated more
on popular support. The results of the two conventions suggested that in both the major parties orthodoxy was being
allowed to take precedence over popular preference.

What kind of person does a convention choose as party
candidate for the presidency? The first consideration is that he
must be a person who is likely to attract votes, not just from
the regular party supporters but also from the millions who are
not really committed to either party. One of the most important
and simplest qualifications is that he should already be well
known throughout the United States; that was Eisenhower's
most obvious merit in 1952. Then he should not be closely
identified with any special opinion or section. The Republicans
suffered in 1964 because they forgot this rule. It has usually
been supposed that it would be a bad thing to choose a Catholic,
a Jew, a Negro, an Italian or a man with origins in eastern
Europe. But the success in 1960 of Kennedy, a Catholic with a
known Irish background, throws some doubt on these ideas.
Many Catholics voted for him because he was a Catholic, and

though some non-Catholics may have decided not to support
him because he was a Catholic there were not enough of them
to do him great damage. It is an advantage for a man to come
from a large state, partly because he will get many votes from
people in his own state.

In many countries the choice of the chief executive is limited
to people who have served a long time as elected members of
the national parliament and have experience as ministers. In
the United States there are few such people. In Congress
senators are likely to be much better known than representatives, and a senator is so well placed that he may not wish to
give up his Senate seat to accept an executive position. Cabinet
members are overshadowed by the President. Also they are not
often appointed from either House of Congress. It is quite usual
for most of them never to have held any elective office, and a
man who has never won an election is not likely to be favoured
for the presidency unless there are very special circumstances,
as with Eisenhower.

It is clearly desirable that the head of the executive should
have experience of national politics and of administrative
responsibility. In European parliamentary systems prime
ministers generally combine these qualifications. But in the
United States a senator has no administrative experience, and
the people with such experience in elective offices usually have
no experience of national politics. A state governor does a job
in his state similar, up to a point, to that of the President on a
larger scale—but he has nothing to do with international
relations.

In recent times the presidency has become so deeply involved
in world affairs that a governor's experience, limited usually
to state politics, may seem to be too narrow. That is why there
has been more of a tendency to choose senators rather than
governors—and recent Vice-Presidents have tended to come
from Congress too. If Presidents become more inclined to use
their Vice-Presidents as close colleagues in administration, we
may see a tendency for the Vice-President to be strongly placed
for winning the presidential nomination, as happened when the
Republicans chose Nixon in 1960. President Eisenhower gave
Nixon a real job as Vice-President, so Nixon, who had previously been in Congress, had all the right experience when the

Republicans had to choose their man in 1960. This factor was still important in 1968. Similarly, Humphrey was given real work to do under Johnson in 1964–68, and when Johnson decided not to be a candidate in 1968 Humphrey seemed to the party regulars to be the obvious man to choose as the next candidate.

One curious feature of the American system is that it does not provide much for an ex-President to do after the end of his term. This does not matter if a man becomes President when he is fifty-five or more; he can just retire. John Kennedy would have come to the end of his term at just over fifty if he had lived, and so would his brother Robert if he too had lived and been elected (which at one time in 1968 looked probable). No one has returned to the presidency after an interval, but it could happen.

A defeated candidate for the presidency may also find himself without a political role. Nixon was defeated in 1960 when he was aged forty-seven. After that he was chosen by the Republicans as candidate for the governorship of California, but defeated at the election. He then took up private law practice, and continued without any political office and without even any definable position in the Republican opposition to the Democratic regime. Yet his position in the party was always important, and after 1964 many regarded him as though he were almost the leader.

All these problems indicate the isolation of the presidency, and the fact that an American political career may follow several different patterns; the presidency does not fit obviously into any one of them.

Once a party has chosen its candidate the whole party machine comes into operation for the election, and at this stage party funds can be used in the struggle. From August to early November the two chosen party champions conduct their campaign against one another, and each candidate has the help of the whole of his party's machine in all of the states (except possibly some states which dislike him so much that the local party organisation refuses to support him). Part of the campaign is conducted traditionally by travelling round the country in a train which carries the candidate and a huge staff, together with journalists and television people; the candidate addresses crowds either from the train or at meeting places near the track. It seems strange that Americans still use this old-fashioned means of transport for presidential campaigning. Naturally, the candidates also make speeches in halls, and above all appear in television programmes. By now the main part of their campaign is really on television, and here each of the candidates tries to appeal to the widest group of people that he can, by appearing either alone or in confrontation with his rival.

The whole business of choosing the President has such a long period of preparation that some of the aspects of American government have to be put into cold storage during the period of the campaign, and it sometimes becomes difficult to keep public interest alive for so long. Remarkably, in spite of all this effort, the number of people who vote even in presidential elections is rather small—usually not more than three-fifths of the whole electorate.

In all this business the choice of the Vice-President receives less attention. As we have seen, if the President survives for his full four years, the Vice-President has no political functions except those which the President may give him. Yet if the President dies the Vice-President takes his place. At the presidential election the Vice-President is elected together with his leader, though the voters take little notice of the vice-presidential candidate, who is chosen by the party at the convention together with the party's candidate for the presidency. Until quite recent times it used to be the practice for a party to choose somebody rather different from its presidential candidate for the vice-presidential candidature, so as to placate those elements in the party which might have been displeased by the presidential choice. More recently it has become usual for a party convention to allow the presidential candidate to choose his own colleague as candidate for the vice-presidency. There is some good sense in this new development; if a President should happen to die while in office it is a good thing that his replacement for the rest of his term should follow policies similar to those intended by the person who had actually been elected. In 1960 Kennedy personally chose Senator Lyndon Johnson, partly in an attempt to please the southern elements in the Democratic Party, but partly also because Johnson

seemed likely to be in sympathy with Kennedy's ideas. When
Johnson became President, he pressed on with Kennedy's liberal
policies for dealing with poverty, the Negro problem and other
social questions, and in 1964 Johnson chose as his running mate
Hubert Humphrey, who seemed likely to have similar liberal
inclinations. Nixon's choice of Governor Agnew in 1968 is not
easy to explain; it seems to have been partly to satisfy some
conservative elements in the Republican Party, partly to gain
votes from ethnic minorities who might be attracted to vote for
Nixon and Agnew because of Agnew's Greek immigrant
connections.

4. Elections for Congress

Members of the House of Representatives are elected for two
years by districts each of which has one seat in the House, and
in each election the candidate who wins most votes is elected
for his district.

This system of election, resembling the British, tends to
maintain a two-party system once it is established. It is almost
impossible to be elected without being a Republican or a
Democrat, but the need to work within one of these parties does
not force a man to adopt any narrow opinion. One possible
obstacle to a person hoping to stand for election comes from the
convention that every candidate must be a resident of the
district in which he seeks election. This rule prevents membership from being flexible, and if a person is elected and then
defeated after being a member for some years, he cannot then
try to be elected for another district unless he changes his
residence.

Like many parliaments the two house of Congress are both
full of lawyers. Also, it has been almost unknown for any
manual worker ever to be elected. This does not mean that
there is a concentration of upper middle-class people. Many
people whose fathers were manual workers have been elected,
but not until they have attained some position in society themselves.

In the Senate each state has two seats and each senator is
chosen for six years, but the two senators for any one state
hold office for different periods. Normally a state chooses only

one senator at a time, and at each of the two-yearly elections only one-third of the Senate seats throughout the United States are vacant, plus a few odd seats which may have become vacant because of the death or resignation of senators.

Before the choice of either a senator or a member of the House of Representatives, each of the parties has held a primary election to choose its candidate. So if a state is choosing a senator in November the two parties in that state will have chosen their candidates at a primary election some months before. The character of the primary elections varies, and in some cases the people are really choosing between personalities while in other cases they are choosing between rival policies inside the same party.

The southern states (with some recent exceptions) have tended to choose only Democrats for the United States Senate and House of Representatives, so there the choice of the Democratic candidate becomes the effective election in every case. At the formal election in November very few people vote and everyone knows that the Democrat will win. But the Democratic primary election often produces a very exciting struggle. Candidates for the Democratic nomination rival one another in their attempts to win the Democratic voters. Sometimes they concentrate on trying to present themselves as attractive personalities, sometimes they advocate particular types of policies. So far it has been dangerous in the south to advocate liberal policies towards Negroes, and some candidates have gained votes through campaigns based on racial hatred. But above all a candidate must try to get himself known as widely as possible; someone who wants to be senator must get himself known all through the state, and someone who hopes to go into the House of Representatives must concentrate on his own district. Handshaking is one of the most important activities of every American political candidate—even more than in European countries.

Sometimes there are several Democratic candidates for the Democratic nomination, and in some states there is a second ballot for the primary election if none of them gets the majority at the first. When there is a second ballot it is usually held between the two individuals who have the largest number of votes at the first. It is only in the primary elections that a second ballot is used, because in the formal election there is rivalry only between the Democratic and Republican candidates. One of these is sure to have an overall majority.

The amount of interest taken in congressional elections varies enormously according to the conditions. A party primary election may turn out to be more exciting than the final election. In these elections too it is important that neither of the parties has a consistent policy. One Democrat may be in a very different position from another Democrat, and at a primary election sympathy with different political outlooks may be important or unimportant.

The position of a senator or representative, even if he has a safe seat in Congress in the sense that his party is almost sure to win at any election, is never really safe. Even a Democrat from the south may be in danger of being pushed out of the democratic candidature at the primary election before the next formal election. Always, in order to be elected, a candidate must first win his party's primary and then defeat the other party, and he can never be quite sure that his party will choose him again. So his first task if he wishes to be re-elected is to keep himself in favour with the voters of his own party in his own area: next he has to attract the mass of voters who are not firmly committed to either of the parties. If he can make it appear that his activities at Washington have brought benefits to his district (or to his state as a whole if he is a senator) he will win votes for that reason, both at the primary and at the regular election. On the other hand, if at Washington he has suggested policies which voters in his home district or state do not like, he will risk losing votes for that reason. A congressman is subject to the discipline imposed by the need to please the voters at home, rather than to a discipline operated by congressional party leaders.

Elections to state offices do not usually excite widespread interest, but inside each state the election of the governor can raise even more excitement than the election of the United States President. But perhaps thirty states are electing their governors at the same time, together with the national elections, so the election of each of the governors does not receive so much attention outside the state, with some exceptions. In 1966 the election for Governor of California excited world-wide interest. First the Republican primary was interesting because of the contest between right wing and moderate forces in the state party, and because the right wing elements supported Ronald Reagan, who was a well-known Hollywood film actor. Reagan was in fact chosen as Republican candidate, and his victory in the election in November was won in the midst of great excitement locally and tremendous publicity. In the same year also, for various reasons, there was widespread interest in the elections for Governor in Arkansas (won by a Republican, Winthrop Rockefeller, brother of the Governor of New York) and Alabama (Mrs Wallace, wife of Governor Wallace). But this was an 'off-presidential' election year; when the President is being elected there is less interest in the governors of particular states. All the same to a politically minded American the election of his state governor—and indeed of the mayor of his city—is tremendously important and exciting, and hundreds of thousands of dollars may be spent even on a primary campaign at this level.

CHAPTER FIVE

How Government Works

A congressman at work

Political protest in California

1. The Balance

Under the Constitution the President is supposed to be the chief executive while the two Houses of Congress form the legislature. This arrangement was made because the people who made the Constitution believed that it was important to keep the powers of the country in separate hands. Their idea was that an elected Congress should make the laws and the President should carry them out. But in the modern world it is really very difficult to separate making laws from the business of carrying them out. The Constitution provided so-called checks and balances between the President and Congress, and the checks and balances have helped to make it possible for President and Congress to work together.

Although there are only two parties, so that one party will almost always have a majority in each house, this does not mean that there is straightforward two-party government, with a government on one side backed by a solid majority and an opposition on the other side. Sometimes the federal system produces different majorities in the two Houses, and sometimes the President is of one party, while the majority in one House of Congress (or even in both Houses) is of the other party. The election of November 1968 produced this situation for the period 1969–70, with the Democrats controlling both Houses of Congress and President Nixon a Republican. Even when the President is of the same party as the majorities in both Houses of Congress there is still no clear leadership of the party in power. This is because the party organisation nationally is so weak, and the party in power has not a single agreed policy. As each member of Congress depends for his election on the support of his local party, and as the local party has its own independent life, there is little hope of imposing an effective party discipline. The Democrats in the House of Representatives often vote against one another, some agreeing with the President and some not.

As the Houses of Congress are both composed of individuals who are grouped in parties without much effective discipline, the main source of policy is the President himself, and he is in practice the main source of important new laws. The Constitution gives the law-making power to Congress, but allows the President to propose measures for Congress's consideration and to prevent a bill from passing into law by refusing to sign it (though his veto can be overridden by a two-thirds majority in both Houses). But in fact the President's influence on legislation is greater than the Constitution suggests. The main interest in the law-making process is centred on the President's relations with members of Congress, and on his attempts to get a majority in each house for each of his proposals. Meanwhile, we must also notice that Congress does not only make laws; it has under the Constitution the right to approve or disapprove the appointments to important offices that the President makes, and it has developed a very elaborate system for checking on the working of the administration. So it is as well to begin by looking at the position of the President.

2. The President at Work

The President may be very powerful in the sense that he controls an immense administrative machine, but he has to work through a governmental organisation which he only partly controls, quite apart from the need to keep a majority in the two Houses of Congress. First of all he has his cabinet, consisting of the twelve heads of departments. The Secretary of State, who deals with foreign relations, is traditionally the most important member, though the Secretaries of Defence and Treasury are not far behind. The office of Secretary of Transportation has recently been created. There are ten secretaries plus the Attorney General (concerned with legal questions) and the Postmaster General. The President recommends the appointment of cabinet members to the Senate and the Senate may approve or disapprove of them—though disapproval is rare. He does not necessarily choose party politicians for cabinet jobs. Some people are appointed to these positions after having been elected members of Congress, but others are taken from state offices (mostly governorships) and others from all kinds of positions, including completely non-political jobs in universities and in business. Some of them are not even members of the President's party; others are active politicians in the party machine.

In addition to the members of the cabinet the President appoints hundreds of people to other high positions in the administration: federal judges, ambassadors, under-secretaries and the chiefs of many dozens of agencies through which the central government has to work. It is not permissible to hold any government office together with a seat in Congress, so if an elected congressman takes an office he must resign his seat in Congress. In choosing men and women for these jobs the President follows the same practice as in appointing the cabinet. All these high appointments have to be submitted to the Senate for its approval, and though it usually approves each appointment it occasionally refuses.

The President also has to appoint people to many thousands of federal offices, to work locally, all over the United States. He cannot know personally about the people whom he appoints to these minor and local positions, so he tends in each case to take the advice of the organisation of his own party in the state where the job is to be done. In particular, if there is a senator in his own party from the state in question he relies entirely on that senator's advice. This process is called 'senatorial courtesy'. But if a senator has given trouble to the President by refusing to support his policies, then the President may punish him by making appointments in the senator's state without asking the senator, and this may weaken the senator's position in his home party organisation. This is one of the devices by which some discipline is brought into the congressional parties. Traditionally, this patronage has been one of the main sources of cohesion within a party. Without it, the parties would be even weaker.

Nowadays the old-style patronage through jobs and personal favours is less important than it was in the past. Prosperity has made it less valuable. But the President's power to help or damage a congressman takes new forms. Much of the activity of the Federal government consists in undertaking projects all over the Union which involve spending federal money and bringing prosperity to particular areas. If a senator is in good relations with the President there may be an expectation that the President will be favourably inclined to plans for federal expenditure in that senator's state, and a senator derives great electoral advantage from being able to make it seem that he has been partly responsible for bringing federal spending to his own state.

When the President needs congressional support he nowadays relies on other methods too. He arranges for consultations with leading congressmen, in order to try to persuade them to support his point of view. These consultations very often lead to compromise positions, so that the President and his assistants work together behind the scenes to arrive at plans which will be likely to get majority support.

Finally, the President may appeal directly to public opinion. The great development of television in the last twenty years has made it possible for the President to address himself directly to the whole American people, and if a group of senators of the President's party are obstructing his policies he can make that fact known directly to the people in general. But this is not necessarily a great advantage; it sometimes happens that most of the people in a state agree with the senator rather than the President.

The President has several special advantages which help him to dominate the political scene. First is his position as the first citizen of the United States, chosen by the whole people to be both the figurehead and the real chief of government. In this he has no rival, and much patriotic loyalty is directed towards him. Then there is the character and extent of the huge administrative machine which he controls. There is almost nobody in political life who has a recognised claim to high office because of his political standing. The Secretaries in the President's Cabinet and the heads of agencies and his huge personal staff owe their positions entirely to him. He can remove any of them at his own will, and is unlikely to be damaged politically if he does remove them. (On the other hand, a high office-holder will not suffer either, except through loss of political power, unless he has been involved in a scandal. He will have no difficulty in finding a good job outside the political machinery.)

Those who agree to serve the President are likely to be loyal to him; if not they would not have accepted his appointment. But they are also likely to be thoroughly competent. The President can take his pick from among the people with established reputations in national, state or local politics or in business or academic life. Almost the only restriction on his freedom of choice comes from the need to include people from all parts of the country and preferably to include in his team at least one person belonging to each of the main minority groups, such as Negroes, Catholics, Italians and so on. But the offices are so numerous, and talent so widespread, that it is his fault if he does not pick people who are both loyal and competent. And behind all these there are the career civil servants, appointed and promoted on the basis of merit, on the assumption that they belong to the administrative apparatus not subject to removal because of political changes.

3. Congress at Work

The United States Congress consists of two houses, which are supposed to be equal in importance. The House of Representatives looks like a typical national parliament with all its members chosen by direct election in single member districts, and the number is based on population. Each representative is elected by about the same number of people. The Senate, with two senators from each state, is clearly not based on equal representation at all. The largest state has eighty times as many people as the smallest, and yet each state has just two senators. One might have expected this 'undemocratic' basis of election to make the Senate weaker than the House of Representatives, just as in other countries upper houses have tended to become weak. But the founders of the United States intended the Senate to be important as the body representing the states, and the Senate has always kept a certain pre-eminence. The President, being elected separately, does not owe his office in any sense to either house, and neither house can remove the

government. With a lower house lacking the source of power
which European lower houses have, the Senate benefits from
several factors: first, each of its members is elected for six years,
so that he is not in such danger of serving for only a short
time; second, the small number of the senators (now 100) gives
them collectively advantages over the larger house; third, to
have won a state-wide election confers great prestige. A senator
has at least as much standing as a cabinet minister in any
other country.

Each senator has a big apparatus of his own. Near Capitol Hill,
where the two houses of Congress have their debating cham-
bers, there is a Senate office block, under which is a tunnel
with a curious underground railway running along it. In the
office block each senator has a large office suite. There he has
a personal assistant, who is usually a very highly qualified and
ambitious person, probably hoping to reach some sort of high
office himself some day. In addition he has a personal staff of
up to thirty people. He receives from the Federal government
not only a salary of $30,000 a year, but also a very large sum
for maintaining his staff, in addition to the free office space.
The funds provided to a senator for paying his staff have been
greatly increased in the last few years. In 1968 they were between $190,000 and $324,000 for each senator, the exact amount
depending on the population of his state. So a senator can
carry out large-scale investigations on his own account to
provide himself with knowledge and material for his arguments.
Members of the House of Representatives also have office
suites and personal staffs, paid for by federal funds, but on a
smaller scale than the senators.

One of the most important characteristics of the two houses
of Congress is that they work through committees of their own
members. The Senate has sixteen permanent committees, corresponding with the main branches of government, and each
senator is a member of one or two committees. The House of
Representatives has twenty committees appointed on the same
basis. All committees give seats to the parties in proportion to
their strength in the House or Senate, as the case may be. The
main function of the committees is to enquire into each bill
that is proposed and to recommend whether the bill be
accepted or not, and also to decide whether to recommend

changes in its text before it goes to the main house for discussion. But the committees have developed much wider functions than this. Nowadays they undertake inquiries into all
sorts of matters and they also supervise the working of the
administrative machinery under the President. The chairman of
each committee has enormous influence over the way the
committee works. In particular he is mainly in control of the
committee's business. There is a curious rule, often much
criticised, by which the chairman is always that member of the
majority party who has been in the House or Senate without
interruption for longer than anybody else on the committee.
This 'Seniority Rule' means that the powerful chairmen are
always old, and when the Democratic party is in power most of
the chairmen come from southern states, because southern
Democrats tend to keep their seats longer than northern
Democrats. This is particularly inconvenient because most
Democrats from the south are extreme conservatives whereas
the majority of the Democratic party, including recent
Democratic presidents, are liberal. So although a Democratic
chairman may be of the same party as the President, he is often
almost an opposition politician.

A committee of one of the houses of Congress assumes that
before taking a decision on some bill it ought to make
thorough enquiries into the background and the desirability of
the new proposal. So it proceeds to try to discover information,
not only through the individual efforts of some members with
their staffs, but also through 'hearings', at which people who
are in a position to give relevant advice appear before the
committee to make statements and to answer questions.

When a committee decides to hold hearings on some question
it very often sets up a sub-committee for the purpose (or there
may be more or less permanent specialised sub-committees).
The sub-committee then holds a series of sessions, at which it
receives written statements from people who wish to argue for
or against a new policy, and some of these people have an
opportunity of attending the sittings of the sub-committee to
state their arguments and to be questioned by committee
members. At the hearings sessions the committee members may
be assisted by their own professional advisers, or by professional
staff members attached to the committee. The committee chairman

has great power over the organisation of the hearings. He has complete authority to place individual committee members in a particular sub-committee or to leave them out. Although every sub-committee must, like the full committee, be composed of Democrats and Republicans in proportion to the numbers of the parties in the whole house, the Democrats in the committee may well be very much opposed to each other, so the exact composition of the sub-committee becomes very important for the character of the hearings. If a committee receives a bill which the chairman does not like, he may fill up the sub-committee with members who agree with him, so that the discussion with the outside people who come in may be influenced by the attitude of the members of the sub-committee. These hearings are often by no means friendly in atmosphere. Television cameras and newsreel men may be allowed in, so a hearings session may develop into a great publicity stunt.

Some of the best known sessions of American committees for taking hearings have been those of the Foreign Relations Committee in 1966–68, in which leading members of the foreign affairs and defence administration were brought in to state their arguments about the Vietnam war. The chairman of the committee, Senator Fulbright, was in serious disagreement with the policy of the President and of the administration in increasing the scope of American activity in the Vietnam war, and both the chairman and one of his colleagues, Senator Wayne Morse, used the hearings to express their doubts about the government's policy. Some of these hearings received the widest publicity in America and in other parts of the world, and influenced public opinion.

Another committee whose hearings have received wide publicity is the House of Representatives Committee on un-American activities. In the early 1950s this committee made a fierce attack on people employed in the government who could be suspected of having had at any time any kind of connection with the Communist Party. At the same time, in the Senate, Senator Joe McCarthy[1] ran a reign of terror by making irresponsible accusations against great numbers of people. His

[1]This Senator Joe McCarthy has absolutely nothing to do with Senator Eugene McCarthy, the ultra-liberal Democrat who was for a time a serious contender for the Democratic Party's nominations for the Presidency in 1968.

personal instrument was a Senate sub-committee, but the House Un-American Activities Committee was important too. Several people who were brought before it or before McCarthy's sub-committee, were subject to persecution of a kind rare in the United States. To its credit, the Senate eventually passed a vote of censure on McCarthy. Many people saw that this witch-hunting was itself un-American. More recently the House committee has questioned prominent people connected with the Ku Klux Klan, thus recognising that right-wing extremism, intolerance and racism are not in agreement with American ideals.

In the long run some of the most important of all the committee hearings are those connected with government expenditure. The committees concerned with this question divide into many sub-committees, and each sub-committee makes itself responsible for looking into the whole pattern of government expenditure in one particular section of the government's work. The same people may continue in the same sub-committee for many years, and so become thoroughly familiar with the work of particular sections of the administration through receiving reports from them and interviewing important officials—very often the same officials—year after year. By this means, Congress has established a very close link with the actual operations of American government, and has built up a strong influence over the behaviour of administrative organisations.

Most of the committees are concerned mainly with legislation, and the main function of the hearings is generally to gather information in relations to bills. Every bill that is introduced into Congress is sent straight away to the committee most appropriate to the subject matter of the bill. As any congressman may introduce a bill at any time, the number of bills brought in and sent to committees is very large. Important bills inspired by the President have to go through the same process as others. If a chairman wants to kill a bill, he may fail to hold any hearings on it and fail to put it on the committee's agenda. Or again he may arrange the hearings in a way damaging to the purposes of the bill. The purpose of the hearings is to provide the committee with information on which it may be able to take full responsibility for deciding whether to recommend the bill to the House (or Senate) and also for examining in detail, and possibly changing, the text originally presented to it. Through the hearings the committee gets a fairly complete picture of the relevant facts and arguments of the attitudes of the groups in the community who are especially interested, for or against, and also of the attitude of the administration. So typical witnesses before a committee are members of the government departments or agencies, or spokesmen of organised groups of traders, manufacturers, trade unions or other organisations in the community.

When the hearings are completed the committee goes into executive session to decide on the disposal of the bill, and this stage involves looking closely at the text and possibly amending it. The executive sessions are held in private and provide scope for much bargaining. Because each committee has few members and little party discipline, each member's vote may be important for the final decision, and thus each congressman finds himself from time to time in a key position for influencing real decisions. The influence of individual senators is very great.

When a committee has completed its work on a bill it reports it back to its house. In the House of Representatives the bill has to take its place along with dozens of others also reported out of committee, all waiting their turn for decision, with or without debate. The arrangement of the business of the House of Representatives is controlled by another committee called the Rules Committee. If a majority of the Rules Committee does not want a bill to pass, it can fail to recommend that bill for discussion at all. In that case, those who wish to have the bill discussed in the House have to pass a petition discharging the committee from consideration of the bill, and that is very difficult to achieve. The petition must be signed by an absolute majority, and congressmen do not like to incur the displeasure of the Committee's powerful chairman.

In the case of the Senate there is no Rules Committee, and the arrangement of the timetable is rather more informal. But there is a very serious possible obstacle to any bill once it reaches the floor of the Senate for general discussion. There is no time limit on speeches (except on those rare occasions when a two-thirds majority votes to restrict speeches to one hour) and a debate on any particular proposal cannot be closed before everyone has said all that he wants to say about it. So if a group of senators wants to prevent a bill from passing, they may make interminable speeches, restricted only by the rule that once a senator has made a speech on a particular matter he may not make a speech on the same matter again. But the length of a senator's speech is restricted only by his ability to continue. A 'filibuster' is an endurance test both for those who are obstructing the business and for the rest of the Senate. Things are made easy for the obstructionist by the fact that he can get rest for himself by various means, such as by asking that the Clerk should read quotations relevant to the bill, and also by claiming that there is no quorum present, so that the number of senators present has to be counted. Sometimes a group of senators have joined together for a filibuster and have managed to continue for several weeks. Particularly notorious has been the series of filibusters by Democratic senators from southern states to try to prevent the passing of bills concerned with the civil rights of southern Negroes.

All of the members of both Houses of Congress are members of parties, but they act on their own or in unofficial groups which are constantly forming and unforming. That is why the President has to work to gain support in Congress for the bills which he wants to have passed. He usually gets this support mainly from members of his own party, but not always so. The voting of individuals is not altogether consistent. All the same, it is possible to draw up a record of the voting performance of members indicating the extent to which each individual has given a vote on the left side or the right side in a series of cases, and there are many individuals in both parties who have a certain consistency in their attitudes when looked at in this way.

The political system in America has had many obvious failures. At local level it has enabled people to get power and use it for corrupt purposes, though the links between criminals and politicians belong mainly to a colourful past. It has failed to prevent the ill-treatment of some groups, particularly Negroes in the south, and the recent federal legislation about civil rights and the attack on poverty was passed only after a long delay. On the larger scale it made it possible for Congress to refuse to agree to the Treaty of Versailles, and to keep the United States out of the League of Nations. But on the whole it has been responsive to the main body of public opinion, both enlightened and unenlightened. And in general it provides people with means for expressing their opinions and arguing freely against others.

Although almost half of all Americans usually fail to vote at any election, there are other ways of acting politically besides voting. People who find that they share interests with others tend to join groups and organisations which try to influence political decisions, and such organisations are probably more influential in America than in European countries. People in elected offices have to respond to the pressures to which they are subject, though they may sometimes react too favourably to pressure which is skilfully applied, just because of the character of the pressure rather than because it is really well founded.

It has been found, in general, that the more highly educated people are, the more likely they are to be interested in political questions, both directly by joining parties and voting, and also through active membership of organisations. The more educated are also, on the whole, more tolerant and more liberal in their attitudes. On the basis of all this, it would seem that, with the constant spread of education, the next generation is likely to be more liberal and more politically active than the last. On the other hand, there are reasons for not being too optimistic. Extremism is most powerful in California, which is the state with the highest proportion of people now in universities and colleges. Extremism of one kind tends to encourage opposite extremism as a reaction. The fear and hatred of Communism has been exploited successfully at various times, and not only by the late Senator Joe McCarthy. Some politicians have gained votes by exploiting fear and hatred, just as some have used the more obvious devices of corruption. The vagueness of the objectives of the two main parties normally allows each of them to react pragmatically to changing situations, but it also makes it possible for a party to be captured by a doctrinaire group. Yet the dismal failure of Senator Goldwater in his attempt to win the presidency in 1964 can be set against his success in winning the Republican nomination. The popular vote on that occasion was a warning that extremism is likely to be rejected in the long run.

CHAPTER SIX

The Social Structure

1. Equality

Of all American ideals the notion of equality has perhaps been the most influential. This does not mean that all Americans are equal economically—and indeed the differences between rich and poor have been very great since the time when the successful pioneers of industry built their economic empires. In the economic sense American equality means in practice equality of opportunity; everyone should have as good a chance as everyone else of achieving wealth by his own efforts; everyone is an independent person, free to make his own place in the world with a minimum of restrictions imposed by the structure of his society. This conception of each person's freedom and responsibility for himself is at the centre of the idea of 'the American way of life'. By now this idea is partly mythical. The son of a successful man is well placed in the economic competitive system for many obvious reasons; social mobility between generations is not very much greater than in England. But the idea of equal opportunity is well known to all Americans (or at least all white Americans), and the doors to success are easy enough to find. There is no habit of humbly accepting an unfavourable inherited place in society; if people believe in equality of opportunity the existence of that belief tends to make opportunity more equal.

The easiest questions to answer are those concerned with money. America has the reputation of being a rich society and it is indeed the richest the world has seen, in terms of total possessions—or almost the richest: strangely enough the wealth per person is now actually greater in the little state of Kuwait, on the Persian Gulf, because of the oil that is being taken from there. Americans are justly proud of their collective material achievements, but the common criticism that they worship money and material things is unfair. In every society some people have more prestige and higher status than other people, and in all societies of which we know, except some of the most primitive, high prestige, power and relative wealth have usually gone together. Europeans of the nineteenth century thought Americans worshipped money because prestige and status in Europe at that time depended partly on family, which did not count for so much in America.

There is plenty of inequality of income and possessions in America, but the resentments that it causes are restricted by a number of factors. The community as a whole is much richer than others, because there has been high investment in industry and agriculture, and because there is a high level of skill. The ease of transport all over the country and the great extent of the individual market for goods of all kinds have encouraged the most effective use of the national resources, and during the past fifty years the law against monopolistic trusts has kept alive the necessary element of competition.

All these man-made advantages, added to the vast natural resources of the country, have enabled the American economy to produce goods and services worth nearly twice as much for each inhabitant as the economies of Germany, France or Britain. The average American is twice as well off economically as the average person in these big countries of Europe. In mid-1968 the gross national product was running at an annual rate of $850,000 million, or more than $4,000 for each man, woman and child.

How is this wealth distributed? The first answer is that it is widely enough spread to ensure that five-sixths of all Americans live in conditions of comfort and affluence going far beyond the necessities of life; the second is that among the remaining one-sixth there are many who are poor enough to feel that they have been left behind and excluded from the great society.

Over two-thirds of all American families have incomes of more than $5,000 a year. Half are above $7,000, a quarter above $10,000. These are the people who, at their different levels, are evidently sharing in the overall prosperity and are likely to be content with their share rather than envious of those richer

than themselves. The same is true even of many families in the
one-sixth whose income is between $3,000 and $5,000 a year,
though at this level a family with many children needs to be a
little careful of its resources. But in general, except for the
poor minority—the one-sixth who fall below $3,000, and who
will be discussed later—everyone has the means to live not
merely adequately but comfortably: to buy a family car, a good
variety of food and clothing far beyond the basic minimum, and
to have a well-equipped house or flat.

But among this great majority who share in the society's
affluence the shares are not evenly distributed, and even under
the relatively leftist and egalitarian government of the 1960s
the shares have not become more equal. An old trend towards
equality has slowed down, in contrast to the period before 1950.
In 1920 the richest five per cent of the people received thirty
per cent of all income; by 1950 their share had fallen signifi-
cantly, to eighteen per cent, and the richest twenty per cent
received a little more than forty per cent of all income. Since
about 1950, however, the movement towards equalisation seems
to have stopped. During the 1950s the share of the highest-
earning twenty per cent remained at around forty-three per
cent, with a tendency to rise slightly, while the share of the
lowest forty per cent actually fell from seventeen per cent to
sixteen per cent. But this figure may be misleading, because the
number of low-income units increased; there were more retired
people because people were living longer, and also more very
young income-earners were living by themselves, and not, as
before, with parents. So the number of low-income units was
increased as a result of greater overall prosperity.

Even so, it would still seem to be true that society is not
becoming more equal in the middle of the twentieth century.
The constant increase in the total wealth of the community as
a whole is being produced by more sophisticated methods of
production and economic organisation, as a result of which
more and more people are needed for jobs which require special
training or skill and a high standard of education—jobs which
are associated with middle class status. Until now the proportion of people with high educational qualifications as well
as suitable experience has hardly kept level with the demands
of the economic system, so that in a free market for labour the

qualified people need to be relatively well paid. This fact may prevent a narrowing of the differential between high and low paid workers. Moreover, as the people who earn more include nowadays a large proportion who have had longer periods of education, so cultural differences are added to economic differences. It will not be surprising if the distinction between middle and working classes becomes more obvious, rather than less so, as a result of the continuation of this process.

In societies which allow the accumulation of personal capital, differences between rich and poor in terms of wealth, or fixed possessions, are greater than differences of incomes. It is estimated that in the United States approximately half of all property is owned by one-tenth of the population. All the same, while the distribution of net income may be more unequal in the United States than in England, ownership of wealth is more unequal in England than in America. In Europe (except where there are schemes for workers to own shares in companies for which they work) it is in general only a fairly restricted group of people who buy shares in companies, though many others place savings in banks; in the United States shareholding is much more widely distributed. More manual workers own shares, and the total number of shareholders is over twenty million. General Motors is owned by over a million people. Many believers in the American way of life look forward to the day when all workers will be capitalists, owners of shares in companies; and there is steady progress towards that situation. Even now, millions of people who do not own shares themselves are capitalists indirectly, through pension funds, insurance policies or trade unions.

The dominant system of values in America is such that there is rather less hostility to individual acquisition of property (including shares) than in Europe. Workers may be organised in trade unions for the purpose of collective bargaining, though the bargaining process is not always smooth and loss of working time through strikes is high, but a large proportion of manual workers have a set of values which can be characterised as 'middle class' rather than 'working class'. Less than half of all Americans are manual workers and there has never been an effective socialist party in United States politics. People in general value their own property, and the prospect of acquiring more, more than they resent the great wealth of the few who have too much.

Differences in wealth are matched by differences in power and authority; and as they are based more and more on educational differences, so they are matched by differences in aesthetic taste and sophistication. Does this mean that there really are classes or groups of people who have such prestige that they enjoy a recognised superiority? Is there, between upper and lower groups, either an automatic deference or, on the other hand, a sense of resentment, on the part of the less privileged towards the more privileged, of the people of low prestige towards those with high prestige? And, to put a rather different question, granted that there are some people who have more power, prestige and money than others, how equal are the opportunities for attaining these superior positions?

Thousands of professional sociologists are working to produce answers to these questions, and they are joined in this by innumerable amateur commentators and journalists, American and foreign. Some of the answers which we are offered are based on casual observations and impressions, some on expert statistical inquiry. What is important in this is that so many people are seriously looking for the answers and genuinely trying to find the truth, not for propaganda purposes but for its own sake. Perhaps none of the inquirers can rid themselves of their prejudices, so as to produce really objective reports of their observations; but at least they try to do so, and they are assisted towards objectivity by highly sophisticated scientific methods. No human society, now or in the past, has ever been the object of such painstakingly serious examination. American mythology may claim that there is equality of opportunity, but sociologists can attempt to show how far this is really true.

In the building of American industry some individuals gained for themselves immense wealth and power, and in the process they had to combine vision, unscrupulousness and a certain technical skill—at least a skill in seeing what people wanted and how to exploit a situation. Even in the past few years some dozens of Americans have built really substantial fortunes by exploiting the market, and many have done this before the age of forty, with or without advantages of family or education.

But these are special cases, and any capitalist western society can produce similar stories. What about the questions which are socially more interesting, because less exceptional? Much of American manufacture and commerce is now in the hands of large corporations which have become socially, politically and economically respectable and respected, financially solid, with hundreds of thousands of shareholders who exercise no power or control, relying on directors and managers chosen by corporate means because of their apparent merit. Can anybody acquire the merit which leads to these managerial positions of power, high income and prestige? It seems, from the findings of ample objective research, that the road to these positions is easier, even in America, for those who start with the right connections, than for others. Even so, the way to success is still open. Some find their way through starting in business on their own account when they have saved enough; most work their way up through established organisations, by showing merit sufficient to convince those who are already at the top. The two greatest changes during the past fifty years have been in the structure of business and in the importance of educational qualifications. The man who starts a business on his own and builds it up himself is not unknown now, but is much less usual than in the past. There are indeed over ten million separate businesses even now, so that one man in seven works on his own account; half a million new businesses are started each year—and nearly as many are given up. But most of these begin small and remain small, and many of their owners are poor. Only a few now build up successfully from nothing. Most ambitious men work for established companies.

In the formative days of the late nineteenth century very few of the big businessmen had any higher education at all; now nearly all are college graduates. The big firms need people with skills that must be built on educational qualifications, and the new generation of decision-makers will include more and more who have studied at business schools.

Although the big businessmen of today are mostly graduates, they come from a wide variety of family and personal backgrounds. Less than one-tenth have gained their positions through direct family succession, though nearly half are the sons of businessmen, and a quarter are sons of professional people, such as teachers, lawyers and doctors. One-tenth are sons of manual workers. Among the various studies which have been made of the people now in top positions we may mention one made recently in the journal *Scientific American,* which looked at a representative group of 1,000 men earning over $100,000 a year each. Nearly a quarter of these said that they came from poor families, and only one-tenth from rich families. Meanwhile, to have been educated at one of the private universities of high prestige (where costs are very high) is a great advantage in the pursuit of a good job and of the status that goes with it; but many graduates of these universities have been able to study there because their fathers could pay. Any higher education is useful, but access to the best is helped by a prosperous family background. Family influence can be very helpful towards getting a job which can lead to a substantial career in business, though there is little hope of advancement, or even security, for the man who is not effective in his job, however rich his father may have been.

In politics great personal wealth seems to be helpful to a man's career. Among the men who have recently been serious contenders for nomination by major parties the Kennedys and Rockefeller had vast inherited wealth; Goldwater, Franklin Roosevelt and Stevenson would be counted as rich by any normal standards; Johnson's wealth was self-made. Truman, Nixon and Humphrey had no fortunes of their own, but all these three came to the front through the vice-presidency.

Some Americans, notably C. Wright Mills, have argued that America has a 'power élite', which contains three elements, first the business chiefs, notably in the big corporations, secondly the political leaders, thirdly the military. Many of these people (but by no means all of them) come from relatively privileged backgrounds, but it is hardly fair to claim that they all together form a single ruling group. It would be more difficult to equate them with an upper class than in the case of similar groups in western Europe. In the long run one has to recognise that in America the great corrective to inequality is the breadth of the diffusion of power. If one looks for élites one finds many distinct circles which cut one another at several points but which are distinct enough to prevent a unification of power or status or privilege in any single upper or ruling class. Each élite group is connected with some particular interest, and the interests and the groups often conflict. The much-vaunted competition in the American economy is not meaningless, and it does something to prevent the concentration of power. Again, there is no single dominant geographical centre, no real national metropolis, but many centres. The two great cities which come nearest to having closed local aristo-cracies—Philadelphia and Boston—are surpassed in importance by several other centres; none is by itself big enough in relation to the whole to set a tone for the whole.

On the negative side there are some large groups which suffer serious disadvantages in the competition for status and prestige. Negroes who have no special education or skill are divided by a wide gulf from the white professional and tech-nical middle class. Some Negroes have substantial wealth and responsibility, the same style of living and possessions, and the same variety of tastes, as white people in similar positions, but for most of them there is little spontaneous and relaxed social contact with white people. The colour barrier is only in part the same thing as a class barrier. Again, on a scale of social status and acceptability, recent immigrants from eastern Europe or Italy are likely to be excluded from the social acquaintance of the well-to-do; it is a social disadvantage to have a foreign accent.

There are differences of status, but these depend mainly on two things; money and job—or in other words how the money is made. Family counts for very little as a factor in its own right. America has never granted titles of nobility; there is no such thing as a person who has high status, or is upper class, merely because of his family, without consideration of job or money. If we try to suggest a prestige scale according to family, we must put at the top of the scale the families of English or Dutch origin which can trace their origin back to the earliest Puritan settlers. Next come Anglo-Saxon Protestants in general, in order of time of ancestral arrival in America. Next northern Europeans; the longer they have been there the better. And so on down the scale, to Irish, Italians, east Europeans, with in each case a great deal depending on the time of settlement. Ironically the Negroes, are among some of the oldest Americans in time of settlement, but this does not help. This scale by itself is of practically no significance in determining social status or even acceptability. But it seems important because there is some correspondence between family background and current socio-economic position.

We can easily point to inequalities, social and economic, but there is still a deep-seated belief that, no matter what his wealth or his job, each man is fundamentally equal with every other. Expressed in emotional terms this notion corresponds with the *fraternité* of the French revolution. One aspect of it is that even where one person does have special consideration as compared with others it is due to his own personal qualities and achievements, and not to his membership of any social group. Just as there is no nobility, so there is no group which claims special respect or favour, and little of the subtle, long-accepted social differentiation which can be seen in European countries.

The absence of any deference to any established social group has had many interesting effects. There has been no accepted social leadership, and no cause for resentment against unearned privilege. More than a 100 years ago the aristocratic French-man de Tocqueville wrote in *Democracy in America* of the mediocrity of American manners, and what he said was not absurd. Now, too, nobody wants to seem to claim superiority, and an agreeable effect of this is the greater informality of relationships all round. Again, with the whole economy based on a free market for goods produced by private enterprise, advertising is a major part of the whole national culture, and though some of it uses crude snob-appeal most of it has to aim at a mass market. It can justly be accused of deliberately re-flecting the most ordinary or mediocre standards on the ground that by that means it will appeal to the greatest number of potential buyers. De Tocqueville could still reasonably complain of poor standards of taste in many of the features of American life. And every assumption of superiority is based on money rather than ascribed status.

On the other hand there are many compensations. In general people can behave spontaneously without worrying about particular social rules about what ought or ought not to be done. Common sense, good will and generosity are all that is required. Many Americans are impressed by English aristocrats or by people educated at Oxford, but they have by now lost their old habit of thinking themselves culturally inferior to such people. And above all there has been a growth of national self-confidence with regard to the creative arts. A generation ago Americans were inclined to feel that their own society had produced little in music, art or literature as compared with Europe, but now the old sense of inferiority in these matters has mainly gone. So many of Europe's most creative minds (particularly from Britain and Germany) have moved to America or spend most of their time there, that many Americans feel their nation to be by now the leader of western culture, not only in wealth and production, or even in popular taste or in scientific discovery, but also in the imaginative forms of art. Naïvety survives, in dangerous places sometimes, but sophistication has a basis which is not merely technological.

2. Poverty

Although the United States is a rich society, poverty exists in it, and the concern of government and people over the problem of poverty has become acute in the past few years. It has long been known that even at the most prosperous periods there have been people without enough to eat, and that the social security system was not enough to cure the evils of poverty. President Kennedy concerned himself much with this problem, and President Johnson developed an ambitious programme to deal with it.

The first problem is to define poverty, the second is to look for its causes. Poverty consists in lack of means to obtain an amount of food, a standard of living accommodation and other goods that seem adequate to a particular society. Exact definition is not easy, and it is almost inevitable that measurement should be made in terms of money income. In 1966 the Social Security Administration calculated that a family of four persons needed an income of $3,335 a year to be above the line of poverty. At first sight this would seem to be a high level to set. According to this standard, more than half of all families in western Europe would have to be classed as poor, and nearly everyone in eastern Europe and the Soviet Union—to say nothing of other parts of the world. The explanation is to be found partly in the general level of wealth in the United States; it is not just that goods cost more in the United States (many things are cheaper than in most European countries; it is only things that involve a high use of labour, like hair-cutting, which are expensive); what seems acceptable in other societies seems poor in America.

In 1968 it was calculated that, according to the standard then laid down, about twenty-four million people, or twelve per cent of the population, were poor. Among these the level of poverty varied greatly, and some (though not very many) would be regarded as poor by any civilised standards. There had already been a great improvement in four years: in 1964 there had been thirty-five million poor, on the basis of calculations appropriate to the value of money at that time.

Research has shown that there is not just one cause of poverty. Unemployment over a long period is one cause, old age another, large family combined with low income, even if fully employed, is a third. About thirty per cent of all people classed as poor live in households in which the father is working full time, but earns less than enough to be able to keep his family at an accepted standard; most such cases involve large families. Unsuccessful private enterprise or self-employment is another factor, when the head of a family tries to scrape a living out of some activity which is not greatly valued by the community as a whole, such as a farmer working alone and without much equipment, trying feebly to compete with the highly organised and mechanised farms which dominate modern agriculture.

Unemployment usually affects either people without skills, or people who have been displaced by machines. Automation is partly to blame, but not entirely. It is true that probably two million jobs are made unnecessary each year as a result of automation processes, but most of the workers who are displaced are taken on for other work, created by the increasing total wealth and purchasing power of the community. To help those who, after losing their jobs, have been unable to find others, the government has encouraged training schemes and given other help to people who are prepared to adapt themselves to a new situation. But in the rural south, when a cotton plantation suddenly cuts its human staff from a 100 people to three, those who are displaced need help—and some local authorities are not prepared to take the necessary trouble.

The number of people unemployed was over five per cent for

all the period 1958–63, though there has been a great improvement since then, and in 1966–69 the figure was in general
around four per cent and sometimes less. But the people unemployed at any particular time include many who are without
work for only a few days or weeks. It is only those who are
without work for longer periods who are likely to become poor
because their security payments are not enough.

Memories of the 1930s are still sharp enough for opinion to
be determined that such a disaster should not be allowed again.
Then up to one-third of the people had no work, many of them
for years together. Caught up in the failure of the economic
system, with only local and often irregular relief, millions of
people were destitute. People who had been prosperous could
survive only by queuing at charity soup kitchens while farmers
were ruined because nobody could buy the food they produced.
Many slept in the streets while homes stood empty because
nobody could afford the rent. Since 1945 trade-cycle fluctuations
have been kept within reasonable bounds. Trade union
bargaining power has kept wages high, social security payments
have helped a little to maintain overall purchasing power,
defence and education have absorbed resources. Prices have
risen, but not remarkably. There has been no long-term mass
unemployment.

Now, most of the people who figure in the unemployment
statistics are without work for no more than a few weeks at a
time. Federal and State social security payments provide $50 a
week or more. But for the people who cannot get regular work
the situation is both painful and frustrating, particularly in
big city slum areas. It becomes even worse when racial problems
are involved, and when a large family has to struggle against
the uncertainties of irregular work in the midst of overcrowded
and insanitary housing, in an environment that seems to have
been forgotten by the prosperous world not far away.

It is partly the high general standard that concentrates
attention on the poverty of the few, and it is possible to produce
statistics which suggest that some material things commonly
regarded as luxuries are within reach of nearly everyone. After
all, less than one household in thirty is without a refrigerator,
and most of the one-twelfth without a television set do not want
one. Among very poor households with less than $2,000 a year

(far below the poverty line) half are car owners—but some car owners do not have enough to eat.

The persistence of poverty in America received great publicity in the late 1960s, and the amount of public attention paid to the problem is itself significant. Absolutely, poverty means not enough suitable food, inadequate clothing, inadequate living conditions, or any of these. Before the twentieth century, by these standards, the majority of the people in every society were poor—and in 1900 the proportion of poor was probably lower in the United States than anywhere else. By the 1960's poverty was still the lot of the majority everywhere but in North America, Western Europe and Australia. In the advanced societies it survives, but afflicts only a minority: some old people, some large families, some of those who fail to adapt themselves adequately to the demands of the world in which they live. Any individual sufferer in an advanced society may be simply ineffective, or feckless, or unfortunate. All advanced societies have built up systems of social security with the intention of ensuring that no person, no family, shall fall below some minimum level of subsistence, but no system is perfect, and some real poverty survives everywhere. The great questions to ask of any society are: how effective is the system? how well are the failures discovered and brought to light? and how much do people care about its failure? In the later 1960s American society was particularly active in drawing attention to its own failures. The initiative came partly from the poor themselves, partly from the federal authorities backed by a mass of sensitive public opinion. By these combined means, much has been discovered and announced to the world with tremendous indignation; but this does not mean that America is worse than other societies in which similar problems have been kept in the darkness, unnoticed by the public and by the authorities.

As lately as 1968 a nation-wide survey of malnutrition was produced for the first time—itself a difficult undertaking. It found that ten million people were suffering in health through inadequate feeding; they were found in many places, in town and country, and the causes of their plight were varied. Southern plantation workers displaced by machines were an important element, lacking the means to move and having a reasonable fear that if they did move they would find themselves still unwanted. People can get food much below its regular price through one of the relief programmes, but they must have some money before they can be entitled to get any at all. Some people are not reached by the anti-poverty programme, because local authorities and agencies do not want to play their part or do not have the resources to do so. Some poor people will not accept help for various reasons—suspicion, pride or, in the case of some southern whites, a refusal to use facilities which are also used by Negroes. Good intentions in Washington are blocked when local forces stand in the way of effective organisation.

The war on poverty declared by the Federal government has short and long-term elements. The programme for the fiscal year 1969 provided for more than $15 billion (in the American sense of 1,000 millions) to be paid from federal funds in cash benefits, out of a total expenditure of $27 billion on various projects. Among these projects are medical treatment schemes (both for the old and for a proportion of other people classified as poor), housing at low rents, and payments to disabled people. For the longer term there are schemes for education and training with financial assistance, aimed at removing the fundamental causes of poverty.

With federal expenditure for each poor person amounting to more than the average per capita spending power of the citizens of the Soviet Union, the war on poverty cannot be said to be a half-hearted exercise. Nevertheless, poverty will not be eliminated quickly because the poor people are so scattered, so difficult to discover, and with so many different problems. One must also remember that the number who would be classed as poor in any other society is far less than the total as reckoned on the basis of American standards.

3. Maladjustments

Through all the story of increasing production and prosperity, the persistence of poverty is not the only thing that is wrong. Some disasters have so affected the destiny of America, and of the world, that their consequences will be felt for many years to come. In one way the political assassinations could be seen each as an isolated and extraordinary event, the work of an

An American family

Protest against the war in Vietnam:
military papers are burnt

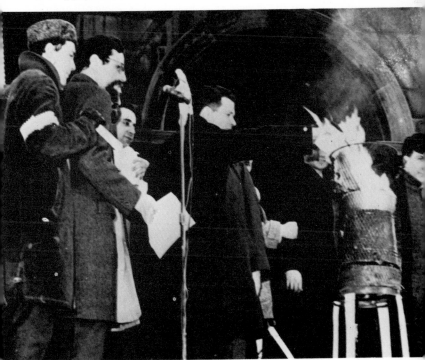

individual maniac, such as could happen anywhere. When they
are considered against the background of habitual violence,
they look less fortuitous. Apart from these political assassinations, it is not only films that are full of violence and robbery.
There are more of these things in real life even than in modern
Europe, and they are increasing at an alarming rate. Crime rose
by over twenty per cent in two years recently, between 1963 and
1965. Nearly 11,000 murders were committed in 1966. The number of murders in relation to population was fifteen times as
great as in England; the number of other types of violence and
of theft two or three times as great. Drug taking and the traffic
in drugs have increased in the past few years, and it has been
estimated that half of the crimes in New York City have some
connection with narcotics.

We hear most about the crime in the biggest cities,
particularly Chicago and New York. Prohibition of alcohol in
1920–33 favoured the growth of criminal gangs, some of which
gained influence over local politicians and police. There are
still gangs, but the old links between criminals, police and
politicians seem to have disappeared. On a big scale crime
depends on high-level and sophisticated organisation. The
State of Illinois, which includes Chicago, has still recently
been worst for robbery, and one of the worst for 'aggravated
assault'; but in many other respects its crime rate is far surpassed by some other, smaller states. There is in fact no one
state which has the highest crime rate for all types of crime.
In relation to the state population, murders are more than
twice as common in some of the southern states as in Illinois,
and mostly arise out of feuds between Negroes. The most law-
abiding parts are on the whole in the farming mid-west and
mountain states, from Iowa to Idaho, including some of the
country of the old Wild West. But the newer west, the desert
parts further south, such as Nevada, and of course Texas (as
well as California) have had a bad record in recent years. The
fast-growing cities of Los Angeles and Miami are particularly
bad. True to its notorious past, the United States seems to
produce special lawlessness in its most dynamic areas.

Crime is partly a result of bad material conditions; certainly
it is most prevalent among people whose lives are unsatisfactory
in obvious ways—people without a settled home, with parents

separated or divorced, victims of various kinds of misfortune, including poverty and lack of education. But bad social conditions, in the obvious material sense, can hardly be accepted as the main explanation for a rapid increase of crime in the 1950s and 1960s. There are after all fewer people suffering from the bad conditions than before, and it is much easier to make a very satisfactory living by honest work now than it was thirty years ago, or indeed at any previous time. The problem is shared with the rest of western civilisation, and beyond it.

It is easy to point to the deficiencies of some aspects of contemporary values. Wealth is unevenly shared, and those who have a big share obviously enjoy many special advantages, including prestige. At the same time the means of obtaining these advantages are supposed to be open to everyone in an essentially egalitarian society. Wealth appears immensely desirable, and the whole apparatus of advertising agrees in shouting about all the good things that money can buy. Meanwhile, physical strength, good looks, determination, ability and readiness to push other people out of the way—all these qualities are praised, by implication at least, in a great mass of material which is served up to the public in television, films and literature. The criminals in entertainment thrillers may be caught and defeated at the end, but they have qualities that are generally held up for admiration, and in real life most criminal acts are not detected.

It is easy enough to suggest explanations of the ever-increasing robbery and violence from the special conditions of modern life. To some extent the American tradition has further characteristics of its own, running well back into the nineteenth century. The old individualism was competitive. It was important to win, to succeed—it did not matter how. The law of the jungle is less prevalent in modern business, but the earlier traditions have left their mark.

Again, the very beginnings of America, and the traditions which flowed from these beginnings, arose from rejection of established rules and authority—those of England and the rest of northern Europe. When Americans built their own public authorities they always treated them with scepticism, and in the early days the population was so scattered that it was difficult for authority to operate. Not only did it lack the support of a tradition; it was in the nature of things rather ineffectual. The police forces themselves have a record blemished by dishonesty and corruption. The early frontiersman had to protect himself against bears, Indians and other frontiersmen; he needed weapons and skill and swiftness in using them. The Constitution guaranteed the right of every citizen to carry weapons for his own protection. Vast numbers of people do have guns, which symbolise their lack of confidence in public law-enforcement. The essentially aggressive and violent elements in American mythology express themselves in anti-social and violent behaviour, both in real life and in fiction. There is much serious literary comment on the fascination of violence and there is a tendency to remove blame from the anti-social by saying that they act as they do not because of greed or vanity, but because the conditions of their life have inevitably led them to it. There is in fact a continual argument between those who hold old-fashioned and repressive opinions, and those who deny that individuals can properly be blamed as responsible persons for their anti-social acts. The system of law-enforcement reflects the general uncertainty about both the causes of the evil and the means by which it should be attacked. In most states the law still provides for the death penalty for murder, yet of the thousands of murderers who had been tried and found guilty in 1966 only one was actually put to death in an electric chair—in the presence, surprisingly, of more than fifty persons and with a few hundred parading in protest outside.

Responsibility for law and order belongs to the states, and it is well known that in some states there has been corruption in the police at some time, and that the system of trial and punishment has not always been above reproach. The whole apparatus for law and order in the states has not always deserved respect. Over the past few generations a typical means of gaining political support has been by breaking the power and immunity of criminals and attacking corruption in local government. Thomas A. Dewey, defeated Republican candidate for the presidency in 1948, first built his reputation through his attack on crime and corruption in New York, and his success brought him to the governorship before he was adopted as presidential candidate. In 1966 President Johnson spoke of a nationwide campaign against crime, but at this stage such a campaign could well alienate liberal support; much liberal opinion tends to argue that increasing crime in the midst of great and increasing prosperity is the fault of society as a whole and of its uncertain values, and that it is to be attacked not so much by more effective law-enforcement as by a reconsideration of the values.

It is easy to say that social maladjustments of all kinds are related to changing and often contradictory values, and there are many attempts at serious analysis of the problem, some speculative, some scientifically based. Here is a society which places great value on personal achievement, on wealth, on the pursuit of success. It is also a society which does not offer much scope for real creativity except within rather restricted limits. It is easy to see how a pattern of anti-social behaviour can seem to offer more to those for whom society seems unable to find a role—the slum-dwellers of the big cities—than they would gain by a docile acceptance of their exclusion from the things which seem to be good and which so many others can attain. Even some of those who can find a role may be disappointed. The right to pursue happiness is proclaimed, but there is much in the environment that sets unrealistic standards. A third of American marriages end in divorce, partly because even for those who are not obviously left out of the American dream the reality of personal relationships falls short of the glossy ideals that are so liberally propounded.

And so the psychiatrist has become one of the most sought-after advisers, called upon by ever increasing numbers of people who, in so many different ways, suffer from the difficulties of adjusting themselves to the complex goals and demands of high-pressure life. Explanations of maladjustment, its nature and its causes, are offered in ever more generous profusion as the fruit of ever more massive experience and research. Meanwhile the number of people who need a way out of their personal problems and pressures grows, and so does the number who turn to drugs. Even if the social evil of material poverty is overcome, these deeper manifestations of human unhappiness will remain. As affluence widens, so the need to make choices and decisions, long-term and short-term, becomes more pressing, and the scope for aspiration, and for failure, more agonising. There is a danger of a solution through mass hatreds, exploited by extremist political movements.

Movements of protest among the younger generation are a novel feature in the American scene, though it is as yet too soon to guess at their real significance. The people involved are mainly students on the one hand, the under-privileged on the other.

Until recently nearly all young intellectuals were absorbed in the business of preparing themselves to take their place in a society which offered generous rewards to those who came out on top in the competitive process and in which the rewards were accepted as being desirable: prestige, money and leadership. The biggest prizes of all were inevitably reserved for a few, but there were plenty of quite respectable prizes too, below the very top. Most young people still accept this set of values, but those who do not have made their voices heard and they deserve attention.

The protest of the young in the 1960s began as protest against specific matters which seemed to be wrong because they contravened the humane and egalitarian values on which American society claimed to be based: discrimination against Negroes, over-violent intolerance towards communism and above all the Vietnam war. The society could seem healthier, more true to its own claims, for the fact that such protests were made, attempting to recall the society to its ideals.

But some of the more recent protest has not really been directed against specific wrongs; it has been more general. Modern technology itself has been under attack: all material achievement, all the demands that it makes on the individual. If a man criticises an affluent society because it allows poverty to survive and advocates improvement of technology to eliminate poverty, what he says is constructive—and this is exactly what recent government policy tried to do. But to attack technology itself may be to advocate more poverty, not less. Some of the recent protest has been irrational and inconsistent with itself: while it is not absurd to shout that America is a sick society, hate and anger alone are not constructive.

It is probably above all the Vietnam war which has led some young people to adopt an extremist attitude which is new on the American scene. They reject the values of tolerance and free speech which the Constitution enshrines. The terms left and right have been used in talking of this movement. It may be asked why then it has been discussed in the chapter about the social structure, rather than in the section of this book which is concerned with politics. The reason is that although extremism is in a way political, it is as yet a social phenomenon rather than a political one; indeed it rejects the whole concept of politics as it has worked in America for nearly 200 years. Some young intellectuals are attracted to extremism because they see the failure of their society to match its supposed ideals, and above all because the men responsible for government carried on with the Vietnam war, and all its horror and absurdity, long after the disappearance of any prospect of attaining the goals which were originally behind involvement in that country's troubles. The established political process seemed incapable of adjusting itself to the changed situation in Vietnam, and the ghastly absurdity of what was perpetrated in Vietnam led to a reaction among people who had felt powerless to stop it by normal means within the context of the ordinary political process.

CHAPTER SEVEN

The Colour Problem

Dr Ralph Abernathy, civil rights
leader and successor to Dr Martin
Luther King

1. Background

No happenings in America are so widely reported in the rest of
the world as the disturbances which arise from racial difficulties.
Each summer since 1960 has brought some riots, and there is
always a fear that racial violence may break out on a scale
much larger than anything yet seen. It is true that for a long
time the coloured minorities have been ill-treated, spurned or
neglected, and that now they make up much more than their
fair share of the poor, the slum-dwellers and the alienated. On
the other hand, the behaviour of the whites towards them has
become infinitely more humane during the 1960s than before,
while resentment and active hostility from some elements of
the coloured population have increased.

This chapter will look at the background of the problem, and
at some of its contemporary features. It will deal mainly with
Negroes, because they are much the biggest group involved in
these difficulties. However, it should be remembered that there
are other relatively new arrivals—Asiatics and Puerto Ricans—
as well as the American Indians. To discuss coloured people as
a whole is not easy, because there is no clear definition. The
term 'Negro', on the other hand, is applied to people descended
or partly descended from slaves transported from Africa long
ago. It may be as well to apologise for using the word 'Negro'
at all, because it is falling somewhat into disfavour, and many
white Americans avoid it for fear of giving offence. The old
term 'nigger' is now considered to be insulting, and is altogether avoided in decent usage. The more formal 'Negro', from
which 'nigger' is derived, is suffering from this trend. In official
statistics the term 'non-white' is used, and in ordinary discourse

it is acceptable to call non-white people 'black', although this term was once somewhat insulting. Modern attempts to avoid embarrassing terminology have produced some absurd results, so that it has been known for the majority of ordinary Americans to be described as 'other than non-white'. But these attempts, even if sometimes ludicrous, reflect a serious intention in official circles to put aside all the factors which for so long have caused one-tenth of Americans to be in effect second-class citizens.

At the beginning we have to recognise that the Negro problem was at first a problem of the south. It was there that Negroes were first brought, as slaves, and it is there that they have over a long period been systematically and deliberately kept in a position of inferiority. Within the south itself there are differences. The deep south states of Mississippi, Alabama, Georgia and South Carolina have proportionately the largest Negro populations, and these are the states which have consistently had the worst record, not only of persecution but also of economic and social backwardness: less wealth, less expenditure on education and social services. The other southern states have similar difficulties, but less acutely. One of the sources of prejudice is social, based partly on fear of intermarriage. The economic and political restrictions on the Negroes have been closely connected with the social prejudice.

Not surprisingly there have been some reactions among the Negro population itself against the way they have been treated. Many Negroes engage in activity on behalf of their group. In fact now, when much progress is being made towards the improvement of their conditions, the progress is damaged by some movements of Negro extremism, and by a renewed hostility from large parts of the white population, some of it being a reaction to moderate or immoderate campaigns for Negro rights or demands.

Although there have been no Negro immigrants for a long time, the proportion of Negroes among the whole population has fallen less than might be expected, because the Negro birthrate has been high. There are now about twenty million Negroes in the whole of the United States and about one American in ten is a Negro or coloured. (The terms 'Negro' and 'coloured' include all people with even one grandparent of

African origin, and the mixture of racial origin goes back in most cases to the days of slavery, when white fathers were inclined to ignore their children born to slave women.) Official statistics of 'non-white' Americans include some people of other races too.

Although nearly all Negroes are descended from people who first went to America more than 150 years ago, they do not share the prestige which attaches to white people who have so many generations since migration behind them. The Negroes were first brought across from Africa as slaves, victims of a trade in human beings which by modern values is looked back on with shame and horror. At the time when they were brought across they were considered and treated as though they were horses. The cotton plantations of the south needed human 'hands' in great numbers, to do tasks that could be easily learned and organised, and the trade in slaves from Africa filled the need most conveniently. The white people who built up the plantations, and made good profits, managed to convince themselves that they were engaged in a perfectly normal and proper commercial activity, and when they were criticised, mainly after 1800, they argued that the whole economy of the south depended on slave labour and could not work without it. Some treated their slaves quite well, but some did not. Many slaves who were used as personal house servants were like members of their masters' families, but the majority, who worked outside in the plantations, were left to work under often brutal overseers, little noticed by their owners.

People in the north for a long time did not trouble themselves too much about the existence of slavery in the south; they had no part in it themselves, and it was remote from their own affairs. A political arrangement was made by which slavery was recognised as a lawful system in the states south of the 'Mason–Dixon line', but not to the north of it. But as time went by more and more people in the north came to feel that the existence of slavery in any part of the United States was a disgrace to their whole country.

In 1852 Mrs Harriet Beecher Stowe published her book *Uncle Tom's Cabin*. She was the daughter of a leading New England Presbyterian minister and wife of a professor of theology. *Uncle Tom's Cabin* reminded people that Negroes were human beings and that slavery could and often did lead to inhuman treatment, including the beaking up of families whose members might be sold to different owners. The book was intensely emotional, and few books ever published have had so great an influence. Indignation in the north against southern slavery became more and more intense, though the south continued to refuse to consider bringing it to an end. Soon it became clear that the north could not tolerate the continuance of slavery within the United States. The Civil War (or War between the States) of 1861 to 1865 was fought over the claim by the southern states to the right to secede from the Union and form a separate nation where slavery would continue; for the north the war was a crusade in support of the maintenance of national unity, but also of the unity of a nation from which the shame of legal slavery should be abolished. There were commercial interests involved, but to most of the men who fought the ideals were what mattered—the right to secede and to maintain slavery in the south; the preservation of the Union and the recognition of the humanity of men, including Negroes, in the north. More than half a million men were killed in the four years of fighting —it is impossible to say how many. The Americans, having left Europe to escape war, had fought among themselves the first modern large-scale war, and one which probably cost more combatant lives than any of the previous wars in Europe.

The Civil War was modern in the sense that victory went to the north mainly because the northern states had greater industrial capacity and wealth. The southern states, in defeat, were forced to remain within the Union under a Constitution which was extended by the thirteenth, fourteenth and fifteenth amendments: there was to be no slavery; all persons born in the United States were to be citizens of the United States and to enjoy the rights guaranteed to every citizen, even against his state; and no citizen was to be ineligible to vote because of his race, creed or colour, or because he had previously been a slave.

The motives of the north in fighting, and the inspiration of President Lincoln, may have been predominantly and genuinely idealistic, but the period of reconstruction in the south, which followed, was far from glorious. This, added to the bitterness of defeat, left the atmosphere of the south full of hate, with a mythology which survives as strongly as the mythological hatreds between nations in Europe. The Negroes have been the victims, and their position today cannot be understood without some reference to the nineteenth-century background. The defeated southerners were obliged to set the slaves free, but they could not be forced to accept them spontaneously as equal members of the American family. Many Negroes made contracts to work as free labourers for their former owners, but freedom did not at once make them rich and prosperous. In the midst of disappointment at finding things so little changed Negro resentments were exploited by agitators from the north, and the white southerners reacted with bitterness and with determination to keep the Negroes from becoming equal in anything but constitutional law.

The abolition of legal slavery meant that Negroes could no longer be bought and sold, that they could change their jobs and were legally in a position to claim adequate wages. But at first they were not well equipped for freedom in an equal society. Few of them had been able to learn to read and write, and the background of slavery meant they had been prevented from making their own way as individuals. They had not been able to share in the American ideal of the self-made man, hard-working, responsible for his own life, and getting the reward of his own work in a society of equal opportunity. It was not easy, when set free, to develop the typical American attitudes. Also, the whites in the southern states did not welcome them into their society. On the contrary, the attitude came to be generally accepted among southern whites that the Negroes were not to be regarded as equals, and even that they should be deliberately excluded from the society of their white fellow-citizens. These attitudes have survived into our own time, particularly in the countryside and small towns.

Federal action has gradually compelled the white majority in the south to allow Negroes to enjoy human and civic rights, as far as these can be guaranteed by laws, but the legal protection has been slow to develop, and it has not solved the social problems. Social and economic discrimination survives but is probably decreasing, but before looking at the many forms of this discrimination it will be best to discuss the more straightforward questions of such simple rights as voting and education.

The first and most obvious device of equal citizenship is the right to vote. The fifteenth amendment to the United States Constitution, passed after the Civil War, provided simply that no person should be excluded from the right to vote because of his race or colour, or because he had previously been a slave. Even now the Constitution did not say that there should be universal suffrage, because people in general cared strongly about the rights of the states, and wanted to preserve the right of each state to make its own rules as far as possible.

During the period of reconstruction after the Civil War conditions in the southern states were very unhappy, and soon the majority of southern whites (especially those who were poor) were strongly agreed that they did not want to allow real equality to the Negroes. Some states even passed laws that no person was to be allowed to vote if his grandfather had been a slave, though the Supreme Court ruled that these laws were against the fifteenth amendment, and so unconstitutional. But there were other devices by which Negroes could be excluded from voting. Tests of literacy were still allowed. At first the great majority of Negroes really were illiterate, as very few of them had learned to read and write before the end of slavery. Later the local white officials who administered the tests could use the tests unfavourably against Negroes. It took some generations before this device against them was given up; it was forbidden by federal law in 1965. Also, most southern states made use of the poll tax, by which people had to pay a small fee to be registered—and nearly all Negroes were too poor to pay for such a luxury. Now the Supreme Court has ruled that such taxes are against the Constitution.

The conditions of southern politics created another special problem in the way of Negro participation in politics. The Republican Party was identified with the objectives of the north in the Civil War, and the southern whites gave almost complete support to the Democrats, so that in the southern states the Democrats soon became, practically speaking, the only political party. The real electoral contests were not the formal elections at which the voters chose between Republican and Democratic candidates, because it was so certain that the Democrat would be elected that the election was regarded as a mere formality. Uncontested elections were common. The choice of the Democratic candidate was the real election.

After about 1900 the primary elections of the parties, by which party candidates were chosen, became more recognised as a part of the real electoral process, and generally they came to be regulated by state laws. But in the south it was claimed that the Democratic primary elections were private activities of the Democratic Party. So southern Democratic Party organisations ruled that no Negroes were to vote in the primary elections. But when it became necessary, for practical reasons, to provide for the primary elections by state laws, they ran into difficulties. State laws were passed excluding Negroes from voting in the Democratic primary elections, but the United States Supreme Court eventually ruled that a primary election was part of the regular election process if it was recognised and regulated by laws. So eventually it was held to be unconstitutional for Negroes to be excluded from any elections, even primaries, if they were officially recognised, and, further than this, that primary elections must be recognised as official.

So the last hundred years have seen a succession of obstacles put in the way of the Negroes' legal right to vote, and it took several generations for the obstacles to be cleared away. Even so, by 1950 very few southern Negroes were in fact voting in any elections. Even when legal restrictions were removed they still had to face hostility or intimidation, so that most of them did not dare to face the unpleasantness that was imposed on them when they went to register or to vote. The federal courts ruled that it was an offence against the Constitution to interfere with anybody in the exercise of his rights to vote, but for a long time it was very difficult to enforce such rules, as the state and local authorities themselves did not agree with them. Federal agents have been used in the south to see that people are allowed to use their rights, and many cases of intimidation or abuse of powers have been punished. Because of this federal activity for their protection, southern Negroes have gained greater self-confidence, and in the 1960s many who previously did not dare to demand their rights have felt safe enough to register as voters and to take their place as citizens. It is only in the last few years that large numbers of southern Negroes really have begun to vote, and their votes may have been an influence on state and local elections and policies.

The Voting Rights Act, passed in 1965 was a triumph for President Johnson with his programme of advance towards equality of rights for all Americans. In the past the Supreme Court would probably have found parts of it to be unconstitutional, but the present Supreme Court could be relied upon to uphold it. Besides outlawing literacy tests for voting, the Act forbids local officials to use devices to discriminate against prospective Negro voters. In four months after the Act was passed, 100,000 Negroes were registered by local officials in Mississippi, Alabama, Louisiana and South Carolina, and in the first two of these states, 60,000 Negroes were registered by federal examiners who had been sent into counties where local officials would not co-operate. By the end of 1965 more than a million Negroes had registered as voters in the south, and almost a fifth of all registered voters in the area were Negroes, who constitute a quarter of the population. Thus at last voting rights have been almost equalised, and this is a great achievement of the 1960s. Already dozens of Negroes have been elected to city councils and to state positions in the south, where such things would have been impossible until the last year or two. In the 1967 state elections Negroes were elected to the legislature of Mississippi, Virginia and Kentucky. In the north such elections of Negroes to political offices have been fairly common for many years, and the large Negro populations in northern cities have made possible the election of several Negroes, not only to city and state positions, but to the United States Congress. In 1967, for the first time, a Negro was elected Mayor of one of the biggest cities. This was Mr Carl Stokes, who had been brought up in poverty but made a successful career as a lawyer. He was elected Mayor of Cleveland at the age of forty. At the same time four of the nineteen City councillors of Baltimore were Negroes; Massachusetts had a Negro as one of its two United States Senators; there was a Negro among the nine Justices of the United States Supreme Court and one in the cabinet.

2. The South Today

Negroes in general still suffer from educational disadvantages, particularly in the south. After the Civil War many of them made efforts themselves to acquire education, contributing small sums of money to develop their own schools, and later higher institutions. Some of these were helped by money from northern foundations built up from the fortunes of great industrialists like Andrew Carnegie. But modern mass education depends upon massive public expenditure, and for a long time Negroes have not shared in its full benefits.

Public universal education developed mainly after the Civil War. In 1894 the United States Supreme Court ruled that if public schools were provided they must be made available to all children, and the same applied to all levels of education. There must be equal provision for all types of citizens. If the authorities preferred to provide separate schools for Negroes and white people they could do so, provided that the schools, at all levels, were of equal quality. And so, all over the south, separate public schools were provided for white and coloured children, and each state even set up at least one Negro university or institution of university level. But after half a century of experience with this system the Supreme Court decided in 1954 that the idea of separate but equal schools and universities had been shown to be impossible. The court examined the evidence of the separate Negro schools and found that, just because they were separate, they were in fact inferior to the white children's schools. The whole system of separate education in the south was denying the constitutional right of equal treatment to the Negroes.

In consequence of the Supreme Court's decision it became the duty of the southern states to integrate their school systems; but obviously it was difficult to do this all at once. The Supreme Court ordered that, in order to comply with their constitutional duty, the southern educational authorities were to integrate their schools with all deliberate speed. The process has been slow and difficult. When James Meredith became the first Negro to enter the University of Mississippi in 1962 he met with so many threats of violence that he had to be protected by large bodies of armed soldiers wherever he went. At various times during the past ten years there have been riots when a few Negro pupils have been assigned to a white school. These troubles have arisen with schools at all levels, in various parts of the south. Many Negro parents and children would rather continue with Negro schools than face the insults and violence which they are afraid they will meet if they participate in the process of integration. Various devices have been used by school authorities to avoid integration, such as getting parents to sign requests for their children to be put in a particular school because that school is 'socially, academically and psychologically' suitable for them, meaning really that its children are of the right colour.

All the same, there are more and more pupils attending mixed schools in the south now; by 1967 nearly every school district had taken steps towards desegregation, and throughout the southern states half a million Negroes were in integrated classes. The first two years of Lyndon Johnson's presidency saw more progress in this direction than any other period, but the progress may be losing its momentum. Meanwhile the social separation between whites and Negroes in the south is so great that it cannot be easy to establish ordinary personal relations across such a barrier without awkwardness.

In the northern states the schools have been integrated for a long time, but this does not mean that all children in the north are accustomed to a general unselfconscious mixing of races. Negroes are concentrated in certain parts, mainly in the central areas of big cities, and many schools in such districts have almost entirely Negro pupils, just because they serve Negro populations. On the other hand, and for the same reasons, many schools in districts outside central city areas have no Negro pupils. But integration exists in theory, and is rather more real in universities.

Laws about desegregation have not touched two other problems of Negro education: the difficulty which faces most Negroes in attempts to get higher education, and the conditions which most Negro children have at home. A family with many children, living in an overcrowded and noisy apartment, surrounded by people who are demoralised by lack of opportunity and by southern white hostility or northern indifference cannot easily send a son to university or give him good conditions in which to study. For a Negro from a poor family to pass through a university or professional training course demands exceptional persistence and devotion. Even so, more than 200,000 Negro students are now in higher education; that means a proportion well under half of that among white Americans, but much higher than that among British people.

Freedom from slavery did not bring the southern Negroes much confidence that they would be properly treated in matters connected with law enforcement. The powers of the states are so extensive under the Constitution that it is very difficult for the central authorities to protect people against local injustice. Law and order are the responsibility of the state, so any case of theft or murder or rape is dealt with by local authorities under state jurisdiction. The local police arrest suspects, who are tried in local courts. If found guilty they pay their fines to local authorities, and the prisons are under local control. Federal police, courts and prisons are concerned only with enforcing federal laws.

The local authorities in the south reflect the popular prejudices against Negroes, and for a long time there were many cases of injustice. In the 1930s the federal authorities began to take an interest in these matters in an effective way. The Constitution, including its fourteenth amendment, provided the doctrine that the right to a fair trial was a federal right, so if a person complained that a local trial had been improperly conducted, the federal authorities could look into the complaint. Federal laws provided some means of ensuring that local justice was properly carried out. The federal authorities investigated some trials of Negroes and found them to be improper, because the people accused had been questioned improperly to induce them to confess, or because Negroes had been systematically excluded from juries. Even so, the federal courts could only declare a trial to have been null and void. Local authorities could then bring the accused person to trial again.

Also, the local authorities have often been slow to charge any white person with an offence against a Negro. A policeman arrested a Negro on suspicion that he had stolen a tyre, and then beat him so badly that he died; the local authorities would not charge him with homicide, but he was given a long prison sentence in a federal court for the federal offence of not respecting the Negro's federal right to proper treatment as a suspect. All these actions by the federal authorities have been very effective in improving the administration of justice by southern local authorities, which have recently shown themselves more ready to arrest and punish white people for offences against Negroes.

The terrible practice of lynching was common in the south fifty or sixty years ago, but has by now disappeared. In the bad days of lynching an angry mob of white people would often force its way into a police station to get hold of a Negro who had been arrested, drag him out and kill him in the street. Lynching expressed an attitude derived from the frontier and its mythology—the idea that individual or group action was more valid than the action of constituted public authorities. Jungle law has a certain attraction. It is even now very easy to buy a gun, and the Constitution gives each man the right to have weapons for his own protection. But what made lynching particularly horrible was its use against Negroes, symbolising the subjection through terror of the Negro population. No white people were ever punished for taking part in a lynching.

Although the old-style lynchings do not happen any more, the Ku Klux Klan still operates. This was formed in its present form in 1915 as an irregular organisation of southern whites devoted to maintaining white supremacy through terror, with the subsidiary purpose of persecuting Jews and Catholics. Members meet from time to time for hate rallies, dressed in white cloaks and hoods which create an atmosphere of sinister mystery. In many cases people holding public offices, including offices connected with law enforcement, have actually been members of the Klan themselves, and the authorities in the deep south have tended to be either afraid of it or actively sympathetic to it. Recently the Klan has begun to be active on a small scale in a few northern states as well as the south, but on the whole its power has probably tended to decrease. Important signs of the new strength of enlightened thought are President Johnson's action in urging legislation against the Klan, and the fact that the Committee on Un-American Activities of the United States Senate has recently investigated the Klan. Ten years ago this Committee identified 'un-Americanness' mainly with the political left, and with the Communist Party in particular; now the Klan, as an element of the obscurantist extreme right, is regarded as un-American. Its super-patriotic postures do not agree with the idea that patriotism involves respect for the whole of the nation, of which black people form a part.

In formally definable matters such as voting rights, access to education and non-discriminatory law enforcement there has been real progress, helped by the National Association for the Advancement of Coloured People, and by the sympathy of millions of enlightened white people. As society as a whole has become more humanitarian and more permissive, so there has been a growing sense of shame at the ill-treatment of a large group of United States citizens. Many students and other young people, all over the United States, have joined in the struggle for equal treatment for southern Negroes, in which they find an outlet for their idealism. But now the main problems are not so much those concerned with formally-definable rights, but rather with the treatment of Negroes as human beings in economic and social matters.

In the south it is still difficult for Negroes to set up in business on their own account, and there are many jobs from which they are excluded. In restaurants used by white people it is easier for Negroes to get work in clearing away and washing dirty dishes than in serving the customers. The vaunted 'traditions of the south' involve the treatment of Negroes as inferiors and the avoidance of all social relations with them on terms of equality. In the time of slavery Negroes did not have surnames; so now, white southern traditionalists avoid calling a Negro 'Mr Smith', or shaking his hand, or doing anything which suggests that he has a claim to equal respect as a human being. For generations Negroes have been excluded from restaurants and hotels except those especially provided for Negroes.

One obstacle in the way of a satisfactory solution to the racial problem has come from the old white habit of regarding Negroes as inferior, even while trying to help them. *Uncle Tom's Cabin* made its contribution to the ending of slavery, but it was an attack on cruel and callous behaviour towards people whose essentially inferior status it tended to accept. So some Negroes have been suspicious of contemporary benevolence.

The roads are open to all, but about 1960 a Mississippi hospital had white parking and coloured parking. When a Negro travels through the south the motels he passes on the way do not have notices to say that Negroes are not to come in, but it is advisable for him to look for one of the few places where he will be accepted. Until 1964 he could be excluded by people who had the law behind them, and even now it may be unpleasant to insist upon his newly-gained rights under federal law. Trains and buses on inter-state journeys have long been desegregated by federal law, and in trains, where each passenger is given a reserved seat, the races are mixed up. For a long time local southern buses were segregated, but non-violent action against the principle of segregation in buses, and at lunch-counters, in southern cities in the early 1960s, had some effect, and the Civil Rights Act of 1964 made discrimination in public accommodation illegal.

The concessions that have been made in the south have been made under federal law, supported by federal enforcement and by the action of unofficial groups who consider southern segregation a scandal. But enforcement is not easy because it is often not supported by local authorities. Southern voters still choose candidates whose main policy is to defend the traditions of the south, and when Governor, Mayor, legislators and local councillors have been elected as open upholders of segregation, and have appointed local officials who agree with them, they are not likely to take spontaneous action in support of equal treatment for all.

In spite of all the determined resistance to change in the south, change is coming about. New industries have been developed on a large scale, and many Negroes have well-paid jobs. In the larger cities a substantial Negro professional class has grown up, including doctors and lawyers who look after the interests of the Negro communities, which are able to support them. Negro middle-class districts in Atlanta, Georgia, are indistinguishable from white districts of the same type, and the conditions exist for movement towards normal mixing of people at that level. Other southern communities are showing signs of similar development.

3. The Northern Cities

By around 1960 it seemed that the position of Negroes in the north and west was becoming more difficult, in different ways,

Cotton picking in Mississippi

Looting after the assassination of Dr Martin Luther King

than in the south. These areas have never had slavery or official discrimination, and over several decades there has been a steady migration of Negroes out of the south, in search of better opportunities and better personal treatment in the northern cities. But Negroes moving into the north have found themselves in the position of the least-favoured immigrants. Most have arrived with little money, education or skill, and have congregated in the worst city slum areas, taking whatever jobs they could find, condemned to a position of inferiority from which they find little hope of escape.

In the northern cities Negroes are no longer a small minority. In some of them the proportion of Negroes is now greater than in most cities in the south. In the national capital, Washington, which is on the border between south and north, more than half the population of 750,000 is Negro—though nearly two million other people, mainly white, live in suburbs outside the city boundary. In Baltimore, Philadelphia, New York, Chicago and Detroit, Negroes make up between a fifth and a third of the whole city population. Each of these cities has some fashionable residential districts still inhabited by well-to-do white people who prefer city life, but as a whole each city centre, with its offices, shops, restaurants and places of entertainment, is surrounded by lower-income residential areas and industrial districts. The central slums are dominated by Negroes, many of whom, particularly those without training, have difficulty in finding work. Negro unemployment in these cities has frequently been above ten per cent in recent years and much more than this among the younger people.

In the United States as a whole there has been rapid improvement in the 1960s. Around 1960 the unemployment rate among Negroes was up to three times as great as among white people. By late 1968 the discrepancy had been reduced, with 6 per cent of Negroes unemployed compared with 3·5 per cent of whites. Among Negroes aged between nineteen and sixty-four the rate was down to 4 per cent.

Negroes are under-privileged, and very obviously so, but they are not really neglected. The city authorities make immense efforts to provide new housing, and employ armies of social workers as well as dedicated teachers; but the prosperous individuals who make up these city communities live in a different world. The great majority have homes in pleasant suburbs outside, and have their role, both social and economic, in a huge industrial and commercial system with which they are well satisfied. Some of their wives occupy themselves in voluntary work for the under-privileged, supplementing the professional social workers employed by the authorities. But there is little scope for spontaneous integration of these Negro slum-dwellers into the main stream of community life, and even those Negroes who do obtain good education and qualifications find it difficult to be accepted as social equals.

The Negro problem is mainly associated with discrimination in the south, and with slums, poverty and alienation every-where. This is not the whole of the story. For a long time there has been opportunity for Negroes to get education and quali-fications, and more and more Negroes are taking advantage of these opportunities. It has already been stated that the pro-portion of Negroes who receive higher education is now larger than the proportion of English people who do so. A nation-wide survey carried out by the magazine *Fortune* in 1967 showed that the median income of non-white families rose by a third in the period 1961–66, to $4,600—a figure far higher than the median family income in Britain or France. More than a quarter of Negro families were really comfortable financially, with incomes over $7,000—a level reached by less than one-tenth of British families. The proportion of Negroes with higher-level profes-sional and technical jobs was still low, but rising fast—from 4·1 per cent in 1961 to 5·9 per cent in 1966. Three-quarters of all Negroes thought that their conditions had improved, and were optimistic. Depression, slums and hopelessness exist, but they affect only a minority. Meanwhile, for the Negroes who have achieved qualifications and prosperity, there is still a problem of social acceptance.

One difficult problem is housing. The old slum areas are the most obvious aspect of it, but not the whole. Two-fifths of all Negroes own their own houses. But a Negro who has the means to live as a secure, well-placed citizen, may find difficulty in getting a home in the place which he would prefer. It can happen that if a Negro moves into a house in a white area his white neighbours panic and move out, fearing that the presence of coloured people must bring the district down. Some housing areas have changed from white to coloured within the space of a few years. Because of this well-known fact some owners put restrictive covenants on property, under which a purchaser agrees that a house will not be sold or rented to a Negro. This has led to a wholesale exclusion of Negroes from the possibility of living in the best districts, particularly in suburbs. The latest civil rights legislation proposed by President Johnson in 1965–66 began to try to deal with this problem by partially forbidding those restrictions, but it was unpopular with most white opinion in the north, partly because it interfered with a man's freedom to dispose of his property as he wished. The bill failed to pass the Senate in 1966, but in 1968 the Congress at last passed a Civil Rights Bill which included a provision forbidding discrimination by any person in the business of buying and selling houses.

President Johnson's civil rights programme has had some real effect. The Anti-Poverty Act of 1964 was not passed for the benefit of Negroes in particular, but they should be the main beneficiaries. The Office of Economic Opportunity, which the new law set up, was given power to finance work experience programmes and loans to small businesses, and federal Housing Acts of 1964 and 1965 are speeding up the elimination of slums. Many Negroes have been able to find jobs after retraining. In 1965 a new Federal Equal Employment Commission was set up, to ensure that people looking for work should not be discriminated against because of their colour. The commission has power to look into complaints of such discrimination, and it sets guide-lines which employers must follow. Hundreds of companies have joined in the Plans for Progress programme, which is aimed at getting more Negroes into jobs and improving their prospects of promotion. Meanwhile, the Federal Government itself has increased the number of its Negro employees, particularly in high-level jobs. There are several Negroes in political offices just below cabinet level, or as federal judges or ambassadors.

But all this activity under the programmes of Presidents Kennedy and Johnson lost some of its momentum because of the cost of the Vietnam war. Apart from this political setback, the fundamental difficulties are still far from being cured. The main stream of white citizens are remote from the Negro slums.

They have no pressing concern about housing or their material needs.

Similarly, many northern white parents have a prejudice against sending their children to school with Negroes. Schools are fully desegregated, but in many cases the only way to have the children really mixed is by forcing children to attend schools far from their homes. In a mainly Negro neighbourhood the children are mainly Negro, and in a white suburb they are white. White parents living in a comfortable district who are told that for the sake of integration their children must be taken by bus to a school in a Negro district, are not likely to be pleased; indeed nobody, black or white, parent or child, likes unnecessary long journeys to school. This solution is sure to cause so much trouble that it is not adopted. Integration is not achieved only by law.

So Negroes who have moved to the north are in some ways worse off than those who have stayed in the south. They are much more obviously outsiders in communities where they have no accepted role. Some live in wretched conditions which they cannot escape, and the prosperity which they see nearby makes their situation all the worse. They are the object of much well-meaning social work, and of a continuous outpouring of social analysis and documentation; but it is not very encouraging to be regarded only as a 'problem'.

It is not surprising that the Negro districts are full of crime and violence, and never very far from mass outbreaks of dis-content. Many northern cities have had serious riots, often sparked off by some small incident, in which senseless damage is done to people and property, and the police in trying to restore order have had to use force. But police violence may not always succeed in pacifying an angry mob before it causes more violence in its turn. In 1966 trouble of this type spread west to Los Angeles, where a much smaller Negro community suffers similar frustrations. These happenings receive immense pub-licity all over the world. Unfortunately the public mind tends to confuse these ferocious outbreaks, which have no positive purpose or plan, with the planned and deliberate campaigns of non-violent action in support of specific human rights in the south. For all the analysing of the northern outbursts by professional sociologists, most white public opinion tends to see them simply in terms of senseless destructiveness. The good will and sympathy which people are ready to feel for the victims of deliberate discrimination in the south are weakened when northern mobs revolt violently against a situation which is none the more tolerable for being unplanned.

Extreme right-wing political movements in the north have gained notable support in recent years, being in favour of harsh measures against radicalism of all kinds, including all Negro protest. Meanwhile, among the Negroes themselves similar extremist movements have developed, and these do not really help the efforts of organisations such as the National Association for the Advancement of Coloured People, with its reasonable and humane purposes and essentially non-violent methods of protest.

Among the white population there are two main trends of opinion concerning the colour problem. On one side are those, particularly in the south, who oppose all movement towards equal treatment; among such people one often hears such statements as 'let them move towards equality some time, but not now'. On the other side are the liberals who give real and spontaneous support to the idea that every section of the population should have equal treatment. Recognising that black people have not had equal treatment or equal opportunity in the past they are ready for positive measures to help to improve the situation and prospects of the Negroes. Among such liberals there is a sense of guilt: guilt about the way in which the coloured population has been treated in the past, and guilt even about their own failures in not having many Negro friends with whom to associate in a relaxed and normal way. It is probably fair to say that in the late 1960s the liberal movement is by far the stronger of the two, and government policy and action have entirely reflected these attitudes. A great mass of white opinion has become ready to give support to these policies and to recognise some element of guilt in the things that have been done in the past.

Some recent black reaction to the liberalising policy has not been entirely in sympathy with it. In the early 1960s activists in support of Negroes' rights engaged in collective action against discrimination. The objectives of these movements have now been largely achieved with the Civil Rights legislation of 1964–68, and we have already seen that rapid progress has been made towards greater equality. But just at this time some black opinion in northern cities shows signs of rejecting all this progress in favour of some form of 'black power'. They take the position that black is right and white is wrong, and that liberalising efforts led by white people can do no good; that black people should not aim at being assimilated and treated equally, but should rather form a separate movement aiming at black power. In one form this movement preaches a kind of *apartheid:* black areas, but controlled by Negro authorities; black schools, under separate control, with the children learning African history and Negro culture, even African language; industry and commerce run mainly by black people for black customers. There are responsible Negro leaders who argue along these positive lines, for example in Detroit.

But there are black extremists, also rejecting current liberalism because it depends on white good will, who concentrate on negative arguments. These extremists correspond in many ways with the right wing movements among the whites such as the John Birch Society and the Ku Klux Klan. Some have openly advocated violence, shooting, burning and destruction, attacking all existing authority, no matter how it is exercised. Colour riots have been a feature of American city life for a long time, but some of the recent ones have taken on a new appearance. When people riot against unjust discrimination those who are sympathetic can pursue policies aimed at removing the causes of their discontent. But when they riot against the whole nature of society and all its values, it is not easy to take measures in support. There are some elements among white people, particularly among the young and some groups of intellectuals, who identify themselves with the wholly alienated black groups, and join them in attacking and rejecting the nature of society. In rejecting all social responsibility and participation in the world as it works these groups have little to put in its place, and it is not easy to see how black power can reasonably be established in a society where one-tenth of the people are black.

These contradictions in black attitudes are creating difficulties for the liberalising movement, and it may be that negative and alienated manifestations will in time obstruct the healthy trend towards assimilating Negroes into the main stream of American society. It will be tragic if this happens, and current prospects are not encouraging. White extremists who look to harsh repression as a solution find more support when the public is confronted with black power, irrationalism and hate. Liberalising authorities may be diverted from their humane purposes when their actions are rejected, and when they are obliged to concentrate on dealing with present violence, rather than on constructive measures.

CHAPTER EIGHT

Education

1. Primary and Secondary Schools

America has had a great respect for education from its earliest times. Education is now the most important factor in determining a person's social role and economic prospects. Universities were founded in the earliest days of the settlers who had come across from England. Harvard College was founded in 1636, only fifteen years after the Pilgrim Fathers had landed, and there were eight other colleges before 1776, though for a long time they had few students. Religious bodies were very active in developing elementary and secondary schools, and soon after 1800 progress was made in the north-east towards universal education paid for from taxes. Except in the south, America was before Europe in providing schools for all children, and more recently in providing free education up to the age of eighteen.

Under the United States Constitution the Federal government has no power to make laws in the field of education; each state is fully responsible within its own territory. The Federal government can give financial help, and new laws have vastly increased its powers to help in this field. The Department of Health, Education and Welfare, headed by a member of the Cabinet, is responsible for these functions at federal level, and some idea of the scale of its recent activities is shown by the fact that in 1964–67 the annual budget of that department rose from $7 million to $13 million, though only part of this was devoted to education. A new Elementary and Secondary Education Act has made possible federal expenditures of $3,000 million.

Each state has an educational administration, not subject to federal control, and the state authorities lay down general

principles concerning the organisation of schools and such
matters as the ages of compulsory education. Schools are provided and managed by local community boards of education,
whose members are elected. A fairly large city has a board of
its own, and otherwise a board may cover the area of a county
or of several local communities. All states have for some time
had compulsory school-attendance up to the age of sixteen,
and some beyond that, but the laws are not everywhere enforced with the same vigour. With so much local control the
standards of education provided in different parts of the United
States are by no means uniform. In the south the authorities
spend much less per pupil than in most other parts; more people
are illiterate (having attended school irregularly or not at all,
in spite of the law), more leave school early, fewer go to universities. Another complication is that in the old parts of the
north-east there is more private education than in the mid-west
or far-west.

Most children attend mixed schools, with boys and girls
together all through the school time up to the age of eighteen,
though there are a few separate schools for the older pupils.
All education in nearly all parts of the United States is comprehensive, in that there is no selection of children who attend
full scale secondary schools. This is not necessary because any
child may attend a school up to the age of eighteen free of
charge if he wants to. Distinctions within the educational
system are based in part on racial segregation, in part on the
use of private institutions by the few who can pay for them and
think it worth while to do so, and, more important, on the
different social characteristics of the areas in which schools
are placed.

Elementary education begins at the age of six. At this stage
nearly all the teachers are women, mostly married. The atmosphere is usually very friendly, and the teachers have for a long
time now accepted the idea that the important thing is to make
the children happy and interested. The old rigid and
authoritarian methods of education were discredited in
America rather a long time ago—so much so that many people
now think that they have gone too far in the direction of trying
to make children happy and interested rather than giving them
actual instruction.

School and home are closely linked, and there is, ideally at least, a sense of partnership between teachers and parents. In some places it is the practice for the teacher to stay in the classroom for half an hour at the end of the school day, to be available for any parent who wishes to come to talk to her about a child, and there is no need for the parent to make any kind of formal arrangements with the head teacher before going to see the class teacher. There is little sign of the bureaucratic barriers which protect authority in England, and Parent-Teachers Associations are living organisations through which parents play a large part in discussing school affairs and activities.

Children who have some distance to travel from home each day are provided with transport in bright yellow vehicles decorated with the words 'school bus' in enormous letters along their sides. When the school bus stops all other traffic must stop. It flashes lights and waves arms marked 'stop' to make this absolutely clear. Thus the children, while being themselves protected, daily see the community impose on itself a well-justified and symbolically dramatised discipline.

Instruction about road safety and traffic discipline is one part of the business of 'socialising' the children; the various rather crude devices for building up their sense of being American are another part. For many years children have begun their school day in the classroom with the flag salute. One child holds up the United States flag and all recite together: 'I pledge my allegiance to the flag of the United States of America and to the Republic for which it stands, one nation, under God, indivisible, with liberty and justice for all.' This has caused trouble. Twenty years ago a Jehovah's Witness would not allow his children to take part in this exercise, because he said it was 'bowing down before a graven image', and so against the Second Commandment of Moses. There were legal proceedings and eventually the United States Supreme Court decided that under the Constitution a parent had the right to stop his child from doing the flag salute. In general, however, even liberals have thought it right for the school system to build up 'American-ness', especially because many children have foreign-born parents. But recently the flag salute has been criticised, and the use of religious prayers in public schools has been declared to be against the federal Constitution.

The social education of children goes much further than this and tries to make them accept the need for human beings in a society to work together for their common good in all sorts of ways. The emphasis is on co-operation rather than competition throughout most of this process. This may seem curious, in view of the general ideas that American society is highly competitive, but the need for making people sociable in this sense has come to be regarded as one of the main functions of education. In spite of all this most Americans do grow up with competitive ideas, and obviously quite a few as criminals, but it is not fair to say that the system fails. It probably does succeed in making people sociable and ready to help one another both in material ways and through kindness and friendliness. Kindness is one of the main characteristics of the American school system. Some people think that it has gone too far.

Although there is so much diversity in the control and organisation of schools, there is a good deal of uniformity in the arrangement of classes. In this respect American school education does not suffer from the great confusion which is to be found in England. In America everyone knows what is meant by first grade, second grade and so on. Education begins at the age of six with the first grade, and continues through to the twelfth grade, with one grade for each year.

The teaching profession is not quite so simply arranged. It may be difficult for a teacher to get his qualifications from one state recognised in another state, as each state has its own arrangements for training teachers. Teachers for the younger children have often been trained in schools of education from the age of eighteen; senior teachers have normally completed university degrees, with teacher-training forming part of the university curriculum at the later stages. Education may be respected and highly valued, but teachers are not. Their pay and prestige, in relation to other professions, are low in comparison with the general standards of Europe.

Secondary education is in one or two stages. From the age of eleven or twelve to eighteen the term high school is generally used, though the first two or three years of this are called junior high school and the senior classes are called senior high school. Where the local population is big enough the senior high schools may be separate institutions.

America is remarkable for the number of people who stay at school until they are eighteen; four-fifths of all young people aged seventeen are still at school, and more than half of those aged eighteen. As full high school education up to the age of eighteen is available to everyone there is no problem about gaining admission to a senior high school, though in some places there are selective schools or classes for children who show special academic ability. The idea of total equality of opportunity for all people creates a barrier against such segregation, though there are inevitably many people, particularly in the educational world, who think that such segregation is really desirable, and current opinion is mainly in favour of some selectivity on academic grounds.

Once a child has reached high school he is very conscious of the need to obtain good marks in his high school work if he wishes to go on to a university of high reputation. Some universities are very selective in their admission, while others will admit any students provided that they have passed through all of the high school courses up to the final or twelfth grade, even if they have obtained rather low minimum pass marks in their high school courses. In this matter of admission there is great difference between universities.

High schools generally organise much activity outside the classroom. Many high schools are very large, with more than a thousand pupils, and they tend to have many societies to which the pupils may belong. For example, they may have large orchestras and brass bands, and there is also organised school sport. Every large high school has its football team and also teams for basket-ball, baseball and other sports. The football team is perhaps the most important, and when it plays it is supported by cheer-leaders and a brass band, and by great numbers of fellow-pupils.

One of the characteristics of high school education is its great breadth. Pupils do not specialise in any particular direction, and they take classes in all kinds of subjects all through the high school period. They are given an immense choice of academic and non-academic courses. Sometimes pupils complain that the progress is very slow and that they do not learn very much, but this is a factor connected with the inclusion of children of all levels of academic ability in the same school and in the same class. Children who are rather backward in learning are often allowed to go on to the next grade even though their work suggests that they should repeat a grade.

Although the state school systems are intended to provide equal opportunity for all, there are inevitably great differences between schools because people want to live in an area which they find appropriate to their social and economic position. The central areas of large cities have by now mainly become unfashionable for residence, and many high schools in these central city areas include large proportions of pupils who may be rather reluctant to go to school at all. Juvenile delinquency is very high among pupils in schools of this type, and teachers often have a very difficult job. Much has been written on the question of how a teacher should try to gain the positive interest of unco-operative pupils.

Because many city centre high schools have a reputation for roughness, middle class parents are anxious to place their children in schools in which a different atmosphere will predominate. Such people tend to live in suburbs, and a suburban high school is likely to be dominated by pupils striving towards university entrance. In a survey made recently among high school pupils in a district near a city, in the mid-west, the great majority of the pupils claimed that their main concern in life was with their school work in trying to obtain university admission. Although the high schools are themselves not inclined to drive the pupils to work, students who are very anxious to win good university places are nevertheless the victims of great pressure, whether they are dominated by a desire to go on to successful careers or merely by a wish to please their parents.

Although the public schools are generally well equipped, private schools are becoming popular with well-to-do parents who think that the public school will not provide the atmosphere which they think desirable for their children. The development of private school education is connected with the tendency for American society to become somewhat more stratified than it used to be.

2. Higher Education

For a very long time America has led the world in higher
education, quantitatively at least. In 1825 England still had
only two universities, Oxford and Cambridge. The United States
already had over fifty colleges for a smaller population. By
now, in addition to hundreds of junior colleges (with two-year
courses), teachers' colleges and special schools, there are over
2,000 universities, colleges or other such institutions, big and
small, public and private, famous and obscure. Rapid development of higher education, a common feature in contemporary
societies, is continuing at such a rate that America looks like
being far ahead of Europe for a very long time. The growing
demand for highly-qualified people, in an ever-more-complex
modern society, and the declining opportunities for the less
well-qualified, together with the growth in the total numbers of
young people caused by the high birth-rate around 1950–60, will
bring the total number of students to ten million by the 1970s.
There were more than six million in 1968. Already a third of
the nineteen-year-olds are in full-time higher education in most
of the northern states, and in California a half. Even in the
relatively backward south the proportion is a quarter.

More than a third of the total are women. Although many
women who have received higher education do not spend the
whole of their lives following careers for which their education
has prepared them, it is accepted that the benefits of a university career are useful even for those who do not work in the
ordinary sense. There are still a few colleges for men only, and
others for women only, and these include some of the most
famous older private institutions; but with these exceptions
men and women attend the same universities.

With so great a proportion of the young people entering
higher education there is a problem of maintaining academic
standards, and the process can be painful. Half of those who
embark on higher studies fail to graduate. The number who
drop out after one or two years is disturbingly large, though
there is evidence that even incomplete university study gives a
person better career prospects than none at all. On the other
hand, one in five of all who receive bachelors' degrees go on
to take higher degrees, so the number of people receiving

higher degrees each year, representing at least six years' study
at university level, is by now over 100,000.

All this effort in education is very expensive. Some of the
costs come from fees and benefactions, particularly towards
research, but most have to be paid from public funds. The
amount spent in private and public higher institutions is
approaching $10,000 million per year and will soon be much
more than that. But nearly everyone in America accepts the
idea that this high expenditure on education is a good investment from the point of view of the community as a whole.

The first universities were developed by private charitable
organisations, many of which were religious bodies. The private
universities are still very important, and most of the best-known
institutions, like Harvard, Yale and Princeton, are private.
However, each state has provided at least one university within
its own territory and in a big state there are several dozens of
state 'campuses'. Some of the state universities are general
universities providing all faculties and all types of instruction,
but there are also some state colleges for particular subjects,
such as agriculture. Recently some of these special colleges
have been converted into general universities. Every state
university provides education to residents of the state either
free of charge or at low fees, though students normally have to
buy their books and to pay for the cost of living while they are
studying. Some universities are provided by municipalities of
large towns and some which were originally private are now
partly or even wholly supported by the municipalities. The great
private universities have many advantages—age, tradition,
long-established reputations. They are constantly appealing for
funds from their 'alumni' (former students) and often obtain
immense sums.

Most of the principal state universities have between 10,000
and 30,000 students, and some have increased rapidly in the past
few years. Private universities and colleges are generally
smaller, and although they are more numerous than public
institutions they have a smaller total number of students than
those in public institutions. The private colleges vary very
much in standards and reputation, from the world-famous and
select to the cranky and the obscure.

There are also many junior colleges to which students may

*A modern school-building in
California*

*Student demonstrators at Berkeley
University, California*

be admitted at the end of their high school career, providing only the first two years of university work. By 1964 there were nearly 600 junior colleges, most of them provided and controlled by the public authorities. The total number of students in the junior colleges was over 600,000, and nearly nine-tenths of these were in public colleges. Some of these continue in full-scale universities, others do not.

Obviously with a total of 2,000 universities and colleges there must be great differences in quality and reputation among them. Many have achievements substantial enough for them to be well known all over the world, but among these there are a few which are outstanding in their reputation, both nationally and internationally. These include a few private institutions in various parts, and several of the greatest state universities, but none surpass the group of old private north-eastern universities commonly known as the Ivy League. Their old social-élite reputations are by now overshadowed by the reputation of their graduate schools as intellectual-élite centres. Their fees are high, but most graduate students have scholarships of some kind.

The best known of all is Harvard, which is situated in Cambridge, Massachusetts, in the urban area of Boston. Yale (founded in 1701) is in New Haven, between Boston and New York. There is much in common between Harvard and Yale, and together they occupy a position in American university life rather like Oxford and Cambridge in England. A remarkable number of the men who hold prominent positions in public life and the big corporations were educated at one of these two. There is a certain prejudice against the kind of privilege which is associated in the public mind with these institutions, and that is not surprising in view of the American ideal of equality. For undergraduate studies Harvard and Yale are probably somewhat more privileged, in the old (social) sense of the word, than Oxford and Cambridge in England, but they are closely followed in pre-eminence by several other institutions such as Princeton (founded in 1746), now surrounded by New Jersey suburbs, and Columbia (founded in 1754) with its ugly buildings, which is close to the New York Negro quarter of Harlem. There are also many smaller institutions, mainly in the north-east, which have reputations equal to those of the Ivy

League schools, but refuse to increase their numbers, believing that their small size is one of the characteristics which gives them their special quality. Some of these are liberal arts colleges, without graduate schools or courses of practical application. Most of the north-eastern institutions of this kind are for men or women only, with traditions old enough to maintain this segregation of the sexes, at least among the undergraduates. But at weekends the road from Newhaven to Northampton is busy with the cars of Yale students travelling to Smith College.

For the most part Americans think that there is some advantage in attending one of the better known private institutions, in spite of the higher cost, rather than a state university. However, the state universities are becoming increasingly important, and some of them, particularly in the mid-west have a reputation practically equal to that of the private ones. Almost every state by now has several university institutions directly under the authority of the state government. Some of these are quite old: the University of North Carolina, at Chapel Hill, was opened in 1795. A federal law of 1862 enabled states to establish land grant colleges for agriculture and mechanic arts, and many old land grant colleges have been converted into full universities during the past fifty years.

In general each state has one senior university or campus, usually in a small town dominated by the university. Some of the best known of these are in the near mid-western states, such as the University of Michigan at Ann Arbor, and the University of Wisconsin at Madison, which is also the state capital. In 1967 the University of Minnesota had 38,000 students in one big city campus. A few of the small university towns have suggestive names, like Oxford (Mississippi) and Athens (Georgia). Many new state universities have been founded since 1945, and the process continues as the states have to provide for most of the current growth.

California has a special system. There is a single University of California, divided into many separate campuses. The best-known of these are U.C.L.A. (Los Angeles) and the University of California at Berkeley, which is a town within the urban area of San Francisco. Both are among the most distinguished of all American university institutions, and Berkeley is particularly famous for the number of Nobel prize winners among its teachers.

Some state universities suffer from the interference of elected politicians, particularly from those who want to ensure that the students are not advised to read books which are 'atheistic' or 'immoral'. Professors and other intellectuals are often suspect because they do not share crude popular prejudices about Marxism or even about the literal truth of the Book of Genesis. Even private universities have to consider the wishes of the people who have given them money and who may give them money in the future. But instances of interference of this type have been rare, and mainly confined to the south. The main trouble with the big state institutions arises from their great size, which makes students feel that they are not individuals, but IBM cards, numbers, cogs in a sort of educational factory, and that the distinguished professors are more interested in research, and in obtaining money for research projects, than in ordinary teaching. The older private universities like Harvard and Amherst College have a well-known tradition of personal relationships between teachers and students, so that students in the big state campuses may be disappointed in their expectations, and feel resentful when they find themselves in conditions of mass-education.

Very recently there has been an entirely new development, in the form of organised student protest. By tradition, American students have not engaged in demonstrations of protest, or any kind of disorder, about their own affairs or about political questions. But since the middle 1960s things have changed. Students have taken part in demonstrations in support of civil rights and equality of treatment for Negroes, and many have travelled great distances to southern states, there to run the risk of arrest for their activities. In 1963–64 many students in the area of San Francisco took part in acts of civil disobedience, including sit-ins at business firms. Later the acts of protest were also concerned with international political questions, particularly the war in Vietnam. From protest about the world outside students have also moved to rebellion against internal university organisation and discipline. In 1964 there was a large scale revolt at Berkeley, including a strike and the occupation of the administration building by 700 students. In the next three years there were similar troubles in several other big state Universities.

By 1969 protest had spread to 200 institutions of many types, including Columbia, Harvard and Cornell, with violence and new demands for black studies courses. Although these affairs have attracted great public attention, they had by 1968 mainly happened in each place separately, without much sign of co-ordination. The leftist groups have sometimes been opposed by conservatives, but only a minority of students have been involved in the disturbances. Most just concentrate on their work and think about their examinations. People with right-wing political attitudes are generally prejudiced against intellectuals, and these disturbances have increased their hostility. They also put forward other reasons for disliking students and the universities: too much freedom (as they think) in sexual behaviour, too much criticism of conventional ideas and conventional morality, some drug-taking. Prejudice against all this was an element in the election campaign for the governorship of California in 1966, and very soon after the new right-wing Republican governor Reagan had taken office in January 1967 it was decided that state expenditure on the University of California should be reduced, that its expansion should stop, and that its students would have to pay tuition fees. And almost immediately after this the liberal-minded President of the University was dismissed by the Council of Regents. Attacks on academic institutions are not a thing of the past.

Many students must find living accommodation away from home, and large numbers of students' houses have been built. (Until recently they were called 'dormitories', but now the term 'residence hall' is used.) They are generally adequate and modern but rather cramped. Outside a residence hall for women students at the beginning of term one may see a father bringing his daughter in the car, taking out of the back a large stock of clothes on their hangers, going into the building and then ten minutes later coming out again carrying most of them because there is no room.

Students are well provided with recreational facilities, both in the residence halls and outside. But a student at a university in a small town lives his life mainly on the campus, which becomes a self-contained world rather isolated from the ordinary community. There is not much scope for students to sit and talk in cafés. Also, meals are provided in students' cafeteria-type campus restaurants, where the food is usually good and varied and a little cheaper than outside.

It has always been common for students to work to earn money, not only in vacations but also, when practicable, by doing part-time jobs during term-time. As the total cost of study and living may be $2,000 to $3,000 a year these earnings are useful and often essential, and mostly students do rather unskilled work. Some students do paid work for the university at which they study, in the library or the restaurant, or even by acting as lifeguards at a bathing-place. Others work outside. One popular occupation is that of porter at a super-market, carrying housewives' groceries out to their cars.

Since 1958 the financial position of students has been improved by the provision of loans by the Federal government. The National Defence Education Act of 1958 enabled students to borrow money to help with their expenses, provided that they needed the money and had a good academic record after a period of study, and by 1965, 750,000 students had received loans, amounting to up to $1,000 a year per student. The Higher Education Act of 1965 was an important new development, allowing students to receive loans in their first year at college, on the basis of need alone. Students may take up to eleven years to repay the loans, though those who themselves become teachers in public schools only have to repay a portion of the loan. Those who teach in depressed areas are specially favoured and each year of depressed-area teaching wipes out fifteen per cent of the loan received.

3. University Methods

Although with such a large number of American universities it is impossible to generalise, there is a certain general standard which is fairly widely followed. European influence came first from England, later from Germany, but now the influence moves mainly the other way round, from America to Europe.

Normally a student must attend a certain number of courses in order to graduate, and each course which he attends gives

him a credit which he may count towards a degree. In many
cases university terms follow essentially the German pattern
with two semesters in each year, and each course lasts for a
semester. Under this system the total work for a degree may
consist of thirty-six courses each lasting for one semester.
A typical course consists of three classes per week for fifteen
weeks; while attending a university a student will probably
attend four or five courses during each semester. Normally a
student would expect to take four years attending two semesters
each year (September to January and February to June). It is
possible to spread the period of work for the degree over a
longer period than four years, and some students may take
jobs for fairly long periods during their degree course, thus
extending the total length of time between entering a university
and finishing. Again it is possible for a student to move between
one university and another during this course, though this is
not in fact done as a regular practice.

The subjects studied in a university generally cover a very
wide field. In his first year (when he is called a 'freshman') and
his second year (as a 'sophomore') a student must usually follow
courses in a very wide range of subjects in the arts and sciences,
including some courses which are compulsory for all students.
In his third ('junior') year and his fourth year (as a 'senior')
a student may specialise in his main subjects, and he may follow
courses of vocational interest. There may, for example, be a
course in poultry marketing and even another in advanced
poultry marketing.

In a big university there may be several thousand students
taking a compulsory course at the same time. There are various
ways of dealing with such a course: we may take as an
illustration a sociology course, with say 3,000 students. The
students would be divided into about eighty separate classes,
each meeting three times a week. There might be a single text
book provided for all the students following the course; or,
instead of an ordinary text book, a specially printed course-
book prepared by a committee of the teachers. In preparation
for each meeting of the class the teacher might ask the students
to read five or ten pages, in order to discuss them and thus
find out how well the students had done their work. This is
only an example of one method followed: some universities make

use of closed-circuit television techniques, including two-way devices which enable students to put questions to a lecturer in another room. A maximum of discussion, rather than formal teaching, is widely accepted as an ideal to be aimed at, even amid the difficulties imposed by the great numbers of students involved.

Examining takes various forms—for example, the objective test. On a compulsory course there might be objective tests at monthly intervals. An objective test paper taken at the end of the first month might cover the first third of the course text book and be made up of, say, seventy-five questions, each consisting of five statements; to answer a question the student has to put a cross against the most suitable of the five statements. The examination therefore involves simply reading the questions and choosing the correct statement from the five possibilities in each case; no actual writing is required. The students' answers are fed into a computer which produces the results. Obviously in determining the proportion of correct answers it is necessary to take into account the fact that a candidate who answered at random each time would probably get a fifth of the answers right. Where there is a single course being taken by so many students in a large number of different classes there are obvious advantages in this objective method of testing. At least it avoids the possibility of different interpretations by different individual examiners. However, the method is not popular, and it has the great disadvantage that, while it tests the students' ability to remember material in the course, it does not encourage reading outside it. There is a tendency to use traditional essay-type questions as well, even for comprehensive courses. The more specialised courses which a student will follow later on in his career, in smaller groups, are likely to be handled differently and probably without the use of objective tests.

For every course that he follows a student is given a grade. In most universities every grade is recorded and the record is available for the student to show to prospective employers. All this imposes a constant pressure and strain of work, but in spite of this some students at American universities find time for great activity in student affairs. Elections to positions in student organisations arouse much enthusiasm, and the people who are elected take their work very seriously. The effective work of maintaining discipline is usually performed by students who advise the academic authorities. Any student who is thought to have broken the rules (for example, by cheating) has to appear before an elected student court, which may recommend penalties, up to expulsion from the university, if he is found guilty. With the enormous numbers of students, the operation of the system does involve a certain amount of activity. A student who has held one of these positions of authority is much respected and it stands him in good stead later in his career.

One device, reflecting German influence, breaks down the effect of size. Fraternities and sororities are societies among the students, for men and women respectively, each of them called by a name which consists of two or three letters of the Greek alphabet. Most of the fraternities and sororities have a mainly social purpose, and generally have their own houses within the university area. During the early part of his time at the university a student who hopes to be admitted to membership of a fraternity gets to know people in it, and as vacant places arise new students are elected to fill them. Some students who fail to be elected to fraternities are very distressed because they feel rejected when they had a great ambition to be popular and well-liked. In a large university only a minority of the students belong to fraternities or sororities. Some of those who are outside never wanted to be in, and are rather scornful of these bodies, whose values tend to be at variance with modern youthful non-conformism. Once elected a student may live in a fraternity house and have his meals there, and the meals in many cases are conducted with some ceremony and ritual. There may be some activities and rather ill-defined and pious ideals (some of them crudely snobbish) within the fraternity which demand that the members should conform rather closely to the fraternity's ideas and objects. The main advantage of the system is that in a big university some students feel happier if they are in a small group where they can feel that they belong. Each fraternity has a nation-wide organisation.

Apart from the social fraternities there are also academic fraternities which on the whole do not have any buildings or physical existence, but exist to arrange meetings. Pi Sigma Alpha merely stands for Political Science Association, and is

joined by students who concentrate on Political Science. Phi
Beta Kappa is the fraternity for students who have obtained
very high marks during their course. Local university chapters
of the Phi Beta Kappa hold banquets at which new members are
admitted with the proper ceremonies and speeches made, sometimes by distinguished visiting speakers.

In the past, many social fraternities used amazing initiation
ceremonies for students just elected to them. During the so-
called 'hazing' process newly-joining members had to eat or
drink impossible amounts or perform humiliating, dangerous
and unpleasant tasks. A few years ago there were some dis-
tressing cases of students who became seriously ill as a result
of some of the absurd things that they were required to do as
part of their initiation, and there were other troubles arising
from some of the peculiar tasks, some of which involved breaking the law. Most fraternities have become too mature for things
of this type. Also, they are at heart thoroughly identified with
the established order, and when there are irregularities on the
part of the opponents of the established order the fraternities
have an incentive not to indulge in irrelevant irregularities on
their own account.

Sport has a peculiar place in American university life. Football, played according to American rules, is the most important
of the forms of university sport, but it is only played by a small
minority of students. It reaches its most dramatic form in the
larger state universities. Unfortunately, university football has
become big business, and excites great enthusiasm in the general
public. It is a common thing for a large state university to have
a football stadium with accommodation for 40,000 spectators.
The students can get cheap tickets, but there may be 30,000
seats sold to the general public at a cost of four or five dollars
each. Thus the receipts from a football game may amount to
$100,000 or more, and provide an important source of income
for the university. Even a university in a small town may find
its stadium on Saturday afternoons taking in 30,000 people,
most of whom have driven for two or three hours to see the
game.

In these conditions a university is very anxious to have a
good football team, and state universities award football
scholarships, by which students admitted mainly as football

players receive not only the free tuition but also other financial assistance. The football students are required to follow ordinary university courses, and can be removed from the university if they fail to pass their examinations, but it has been known for pressure to be put on teachers to ensure that the football students pass their examinations, and special classes are sometimes provided to help the football students to pass. In fact the award of the football scholarships has reached a stage at which it amounts virtually to the signing on of a professional football player, and one even sees photographs in newspapers of university coaches engaging a group of three or four very good football players to come and play football in the university squad.

The team is coached by a large staff, perhaps as many as twenty people, and the chief coach may receive the highest salary of any person in the university except the president. But the coach's position is not very secure. If the football team of a state university suffers a number of defeats the newspapers may begin to demand his removal, and it has been known for a football coach to be under such pressure that he is obliged to resign because his team has not done well. In this case the positions of all his assistant coaches also become insecure because the chief coach chooses his assistants.

Not surprisingly, academics are less than enthusiastic about the way university football has developed, and regret that what was originally student sport has become a major public sporting event, arousing state-wide enthusiasm, and having some implications for university finance.

It seems likely that, as in Europe, so in America, more and more people will continue in full-time education for longer periods in the future. The individual young person knows that his prospects of success in life depend on his education more than on any other single factor. So there is an ever-increasing demand for educational opportunities. At the same time, it is generally recognised that even from the material point of view economic development up till now has owed much to the skills and abilities which grow through education, and for the traditional Americans, respect for learning is reinforced by a doctrine that it is an investment that brings the community an economic return as well as social and cultural improvement.

Russian technological success brought an unpleasant shock to American pride. Even the most conservative elements are impressed by the signs that the Russians have equalled or even surpassed the Americans in achievements which depend on a great mass of trained talent and skill, and the first reaction to the Russian achievements in space was a new support for greater efforts in the educational field.

Some of these arguments in support of ever-increasing educational facilities may seem rather far removed from the ideals which inspired the foundation of the earliest colleges, but the effects of present developments are likely to be good. American education has never been specially slanted towards technology, though technology has its place. In some ways it has been used as a device for developing an outlook which agrees with the dominant ideas of the culture, but it has always left scope for individuality, and it still does. Again, it has always managed to produce a supply of educated people who can find a place in the economic and social structure corresponding to their talents and training. So long as the healthy balance between all these factors is preserved, it seems that the present effort should produce not only more skills, whether in engineering or in medicine or in the law, but also more enlightenment, more understanding of human needs and problems.

CHAPTER NINE

Religion

Dr Billy Graham, evangelical leader,
preaches to 22,000 people

Every Sunday morning, all over America, people pour into the churches. Not only the Catholic churches, but the Protestant ones too, are flourishing, and new church buildings, some with interesting architecture, keep pace with the ever-growing suburbs. In England, leaving aside the Catholics, four-fifths of the people go to church less than once a month, in Sweden the vast majority hardly ever go to church at all. Yet half of American Protestants are active church members, and there are few who habitually stay away. Through all the social and economic changes religion has remained a constant factor. In Europe scientific and economic advance and rising material prosperity have been accompanied by a decline in religious observance, but in America this has not happened.

Several explanations may be offered. Religion in America has never been identified with an oppressive or dominant social class or set of political institutions. The Pilgrim Fathers, and many of those who followed them, left Europe to be free to worship in their own way, not as the established authorities told them to. The American mythology assigns its first place to religious freedom and spontaneity. Paradoxically, the original basis of freedom creates a social pressure in favour of religion. Most people want to identify themselves with dominant values, and going freely to the church of one's choice is a way of doing so, and of gaining acceptance in the face of a subtle demand for conformity. And the church is a place where people can meet others with whom they would like to make friends. Religion, for most people, is important mainly as a means of getting together with others in a context which is so little defined that its values, expressing merely general good will, can be easily shared. Most clergymen run their churches in a way which fits in with the ideas of their congregations. People go to church and it helps them to feel that they have a place in a community. Evangelists like Billy Graham draw crowds, 10,000 at a time, to hear them declaim about a salvation that changes people's lives. But in the long run it seems to make little difference. Suburban congregations are reflections of the business world of their members, and real emotional fervour is found mainly in small sects.

America is remarkable now, as in the past, for its attachment to the principle of freedom of belief or disbelief. As the early Americans had escaped from religious persecution in their old countries, so they were determined that there would be no religious oppression in the home they were building up. When the Bill of Rights in the United States Constitution was drawn up it began in its very first article by insisting that there should be no state religion, and complete freedom of belief and religious practice or non-belief has been jealously guarded from the beginning. Indeed religious toleration has from the earliest times gone so far as to take great care to ensure that non-believers are not made subject to religious laws desired by those who are religious. For example, as long ago as 1810 a rule was made that postal deliveries should take place on Sundays, on the ground that it was wrong that public services should be stopped on Sundays because religious people believed that Christians had a duty to rest on Sundays. The legal freedom for non-believers has not led to a decline in actual religious belief or practice, but the contrary. On the other hand, many Americans are dominated in their lives by a wish to conform with the practices and ideas of the people among whom they find themselves, and in many types of social group a person who is known not to be religious may receive a certain social disapproval (far more than in Europe). Modern American religious freedom in the law is often counterbalanced by a spontaneous social pressure in favour of religion, though not of any particular kind of religion. In spite of the Sunday mails law of 1810, sabbatarian feeling was strong enough to prevent the large-scale playing of public sports on Sundays until quite recently.

Development of education in America was much influenced by religion in the early stages before and after Independence, but the government, even local government, had nothing to do with this. Public education grew up later in the nineteenth century. The Constitution seems to imply that public educational institutions should not provide religious instruction as part of the regular curriculum, and the Supreme Court recently delivered a ruling to the effect that religious instruction in public schools was against the Constitution. Churches and organised religious bodies have not opposed such arguments, but have been ready to accept the idea that the religion of each person or of each group ought to stand on its own feet and to be quite distinct from government.

Although the first immigrants were mainly Protestants not in agreement with the Church of England, in the eighteenth century many Church of England people did come to America and brought their former religious practices with them, but not the English relation of church and state. The term 'Anglican' is sometimes used, rather than the not very satisfactory 'Protestant Episcopalian', but Anglicanism has never been connected with civil power. It has some small social attraction for people who find the Anglican Church corresponding with their ideas about their 'good' social position.

Because of the background of American religion, every church or religious community is a completely independent organisation, and concerned with its own finances and its own building. There has been very little concentration on doctrine or religious argument, such as was to be seen in Scotland among Presbyterians in the nineteenth century. In 1830 de Tocqueville wrote: 'go into the churches (I mean the Protestant ones), you will hear morality preached, of doctrine not a word.'[1] It is the same today. American Baptists do not concern themselves much about the distinctive belief of Baptists as compared with other Protestants. Anglicans do not pay much attention to the thirty-nine articles on which the belief of the Anglican Church is based, nor Lutherans to the Conventions of Augsburg. Churches and religious denominations are expressions of group solidarity

[1]He wrote this in his private notes, and expanded the idea in *Democracy in America*. Cf. G. W. Pierson, *Tocqueville in America*, Doubleday, 1959, p. 70, quoted by S. M. Lipset, *The First New Nation*, London, Heinemann, 1964, p. 155.

rather than of rigid adherence to doctrine. There is not much ideology in American politics, and American religion is not, in general, doctrinaire. Baptist ministers are invited to preach in Methodist churches. Exchange of pulpits has been common for many years. At the same time, the level of knowledge of theology is apparently not very high. A sample survey made in 1954 found that nearly two-thirds of the people questioned could not give the names of the four gospels, though many of these same people were church members and regular church-goers. This may seem surprising, but it does little more than confirm the view that many people are 'religious' without concerning themselves with doctrine. From the social point of view it is the attitude that is important.

A Protestant family moving to a new place will probably try out several of the nearby churches before deciding on the one that suits them best, not for doctrinal reasons, but because that is where they find their friends. A change to a new denomination is of course unlikely, but not as unlikely as it would be in most societies. There is quite meaningful competition between churches and ministers, symbolised by one street where there are five churches in a row, all about the same age and looking very like one another, with the Methodist the biggest and architecturally the most distinguished. Just around the corner there are five filling stations belonging to different petrol companies, competing in cheerfulness and windscreen-wiping and in advertised claims of high performance. Here the divided church does not seem an outrage or a tragedy, but just an expression in religion of the American competitive system, with its luxury of choice. This absence of fundamental differences between Protestant churches has probably had something to do with the way in which they manage collectively to keep the allegiance of such a large part of the people.

There are plenty of intellectuals who are agnostics. According to a survey made in 1952 almost one-third of a typical group of students at Harvard did not believe in God, but only one-eighth of the students in the University of Texas, who are less dominated by intellectuals, said that they were non-believers. But there is no massive rejection of religion among the people as a whole or among any substantial social or economic group. A survey made in 1957 indicated that ninety-five per cent of

An open-air church in Indiana

Cuban settlers in church

adults were prepared to declare that they were religious believers and identified with some specific religious group. This is slightly more than in 1890. Even among young people there is not much sign of widespread change. A survey of teenagers made by the magazine *Look* in 1966 found that six out of seven expressed belief in God, and a majority said that their religious belief was becoming stronger as they grew older. Three-quarters said that they went to church at least once a month, though many of these did so only to satisfy their parents, and many had a rather low opinion of clergymen.

The number of church buildings is remarkable for a modern community. In 1890 there were enough churches to hold two-thirds of the population, and, with the vast number of new churches keeping pace with new housing, the proportion may well still be the same. There is still, as in 1890, more than one clergyman for every thousand people—a much bigger proportion than, for example, in England. The art of persuading people to give money is highly developed, and sophisticated techniques of persuasion are borrowed from the world of commercial advertising. Americans give money very generously to their churches, and take much interest in their church finances. Some churches in prosperous areas have immense incomes, producing large salaries for their ministers and large funds both for creating and improving church buildings and property and for helping good causes. But the money comes mainly from current subscriptions and payments by members, and not so much from property accumulated in the past. Churches can be affluent without giving cause for scandal or offence.

There is a tendency for Protestantism to be identified to some extent with the idea of an 'Establishment', and for the older large Protestant groups to attract people who have secure personal prosperity. Just over three-fifths of all Americans are Protestants. These are spread fairly widely among the different types of Protestant denominations. About two-thirds of the Protestants belong to denominations which had their origins wholly or mainly in Britain: Baptists, Methodists, Presbyterians (mainly from Scotland), with much smaller numbers of Unitarians, Society of Friends and Salvation Army. These groups, which in England are dissenters, have together ten times as many members in America as the last of the British denominations, that of the

Church of England. Thus although people of British origin are by now a small minority among foreign-born Americans, about half of all Americans have a link with Britain through their religion, and this fact well illustrates the place of Britain in the American culture.

Membership of religious groups is much connected with ethnic origins, but not entirely so. Intermarriage has brought its complications. The nine million Lutherans (divided between three main organisations) are predominantly of German or Scandinavian origin. But now that most Americans are not first or second generation immigrants, the adoption of a particular religious affiliation does not necessarily suggest a particular ethnic background. The denominations which came mainly from Britain perhaps seem more American than those which came mainly from other parts of the world. Fully assimilated Americans who have more or less forgotten their ethnic origin are on the whole unlikely to transfer to the Lutheran Church, or to any other which has a special association with a particular ethnic background, whereas Methodists and Baptists are by now regarded as wholly American and without any particular English associations.

The Protestant Episcopal Church is derived directly from the Church of England, which it resembles in the form of its services and organisation, though of course it lacks any connection with the state. Its adherents are often called Anglicans. Its origins can be traced to the non-rebellious (and often prosperous) element among the immigrants from England. Episcopalians in modern America include a high proportion of people with well paid jobs and considering themselves to be of rather high social status, but their position is in some way equivalent to that of Episcopalians in Scotland. As in Scotland, this particular group is rather outside the main stream of Protestantism, though there may be a certain tendency for people who have ambitions for social status to attach themselves to it. But a person who wishes to be elected to political office finds membership of this group a hindrance rather than otherwise. Rather similarly, American Presbyterianism has links with Scotland, though its surviving Scottish flavour has been more overlaid with Americanness than is the case with Anglicanism.

The Baptists are the largest Protestant group. From a beginning in seventeenth century England (with some Dutch influence) the Baptists have continued on a small scale in modern England, where they are about one per cent of the population. They also have some outposts, mainly based on nineteenth century missions, in Europe, Russia and all over the world. But in the United States they have their main strength, with twenty-five million members, divided among more than twenty branches, and concentrated particularly in the Southern Bible Belt. Some white southern Baptists, including ministers, have liberal attitudes in relation to the Negroes, and stand up courageously in difficult circumstances for their belief in the equality of all human beings before God, whatever their colour. But the great majority seem to have no difficulty in reconciling their ardent Christian belief and practice with racial prejudice. Meanwhile, most of the Negroes are Baptists too, but this does not mean that black and white Baptists go to the same churches. In southern communities Negroes find their main social centre in their Baptist churches—and sometimes also a base from which to organise action against discrimination.

Next to the Baptists the most numerous Protestants are the Methodists, adherents of the group which grew up in eighteenth century England following the lead of the clergyman John Wesley, who visited America then reluctantly drifted away from the Church of England in which he was at first ordained when he found that it was indifferent to the social and spiritual problems created by the beginnings of the industrial revolution. Most Methodists are united in the Methodist Church, which has a form of service based on that of the Church of England. Negro Methodists are mostly in two distinct African Methodist organisations.

Thus the main Protestant groups with origins in Europe, and especially in Britain, are flourishing, and seem to have taken on a distinctively American character, including a tendency to form sub-groups. But this is not the whole story of Protestantism. Smaller sects from Europe have taken root, and new sects have formed within America, some of them around individual religious leaders.

There are more than a hundred other Protestant sects, many of them hardly known to anyone except their own members, but with a combined membership of more than twenty million. Many of these are truly American in origin. Some are of recent foundation, and the dominant trend is fundamentalist. Four of the smaller sects are really quite large, with two million or more members and several thousands of churches each. These are the Latter Day Saints, the Churches of Christ (with 20,000 churches), the United Church of Christ and the International Convention of Disciples of Christ.

Some of the small sects are extremely intolerant, and depend on a highly emotional and even hysterical approach. Some have shown themselves particularly ready to be pragmatic in adapting themselves to what they imagine to be the ideas of modern society. Europeans are often surprised to find drive-in churches in America. These are in fact just car parks in which all the cars face the same way; you can drive in and sit in your car while the service goes on. The idea is taken from the drive-in cinema.

One might have expected that the Society of Friends, or Quakers, would be one of the great American sects. One of the greatest states, Pennsylvania, was a Quaker foundation and for some time around 1700 the Quakers were the dominant group in New Jersey and Delaware. But the Friends do not go out to attract adherents, and, as in England, they remain a very small and select group, with little over 100,000 members. They lost political power as a group long ago, because they insisted on making a really serious attempt to follow Christian morality, but many Quakers now hold important positions outside politics, and their group is greatly respected.

The largest single religious group is that of Roman Catholics. More than one-quarter of all Americans are now of the Roman Catholic faith, and the majority of these are descendants of immigrants from Ireland, Italy and Poland. While the Protestants from Germany and Scandinavia tended to be very active in building up the middle west after the middle of the nineteenth century, most Catholics stayed nearer the east coast. They were concentrated especially in New York and Massachusetts, and are still a very important element of the population in those two states.

The founders of America included few Catholics except in the state of Maryland, but the later nineteenth century brought waves of Catholic immigrants from Ireland, Italy and Poland.

Soon after 1900 the Catholic vote became important in Boston
and New York and in the Democratic Party machines in some
other cities too. At local level, before the time of modern
Social Security, the machines filled a gap which was particularly
felt by recent Catholic immigrants, many of whom had come
across the Atlantic with small resources of their own. But by
the time John F. Kennedy became President Catholic immigration on a large scale was already a thing of two generations
ago, and the social and economic disadvantages of the earlier
Catholics had been largely (though not completely) left behind.
For electoral purposes some claim to be identified with a
traditionally under-privileged group has some advantages,
particularly when it is combined with actual wealth and
position.

It was once assumed that no Catholic could hope to be
elected President, and when John F. Kennedy was hoping to
be adopted as Democratic candidate in 1960 the fact that he was
a Catholic was regarded as a disadvantage. Kennedy's success,
first in being chosen as Democratic candidate, and then in
being elected President, was partly due to the fact that very
many Catholics voted for him because he was a Catholic. The
proportion of Catholics voting Democrat was much greater in
1960 than in 1952, and with Catholics constituting roughly one-
quarter of the whole population the Catholic vote is evidently
very valuable, not only in the heavily Catholic areas, but in
the whole nation. All the same Kennedy had to win a large
number of Protestant votes too in order to be elected President.
He did so, and in office he also won the loyalty and affection of
the people as few others have done. His success was partly
personal, but it also showed that religious prejudice had been
greatly reduced. In any case, Catholicism in America has taken
on much local colour. It has tended to be not only patriotic but
also puritan in flavour.

Three per cent of all Americans are Jews, most of them
originally from eastern Europe, including Russia. As far as their
role in American society has been concerned they have felt
themselves to be a minority, like the Catholics. From the
political point of view their status has been rather similar and
they too have tended to be concentrated in the eastern area,
particularly New York, though with a very large element in

Chicago. But they have probably been somewhat more successful in the race for prosperity in American conditions. It is still considered unlikely that a Jew could be elected President of the United States, because of the strong built-in prejudices of the Protestant majority. Even so, there has already been one half-Jewish Republican candidate, Senator Goldwater, in 1964. Ironically he is nearer to the ideal picture of the typical Anglo-Saxon Protestant American than any other recent presidential candidate. He is only partly Jewish but it is of some interest that this Jewish background did not stand in the way of his nomination by the Republicans. But his attitude and his characteristics in general are very different from those commonly associated with Jewish Americans, which are predominantly liberal, and inclined to be expressed in politics through the Democratic Party.

There are about five million members of the Orthodox Churches, mainly of course descendants of people who migrated from Russia or Greece or from other Orthodox parts of eastern Europe. It is probably safe to say that the Orthodox Church members are somewhat more outside the main stream of American social and religious life, or less assimilated, than members of other religious bodies. The number of members of the Orthodox Church is not very much more than the number of people from eastern Europe still registered as foreign-born in 1960. On the other hand, the number of Catholics now living in the United States is relatively speaking very much larger than the number of immigrants born in Catholic countries. It may be then that the Catholic community continues to grow through natural increase of population without suffering very much loss through intermarriage of individual members with people of other religions; however descendants of Orthodox immigrants tend to become assimilated by adopting another religion, usually Protestant. There may seem to be a slight contradiction here. In the religious sense Catholics are tending to remain separate and distinct, though it may be said that they form such a large block in the total population that they must be accepted as a totally assimilated group. In the case of Orthodox Church members however, those who still belong to Orthodox Churches are probably less assimilated, while those who are thoroughly assimilated tend to change their religion.

CHAPTER TEN

Private Life

An American football match

One man's work for one hour in an American factory or farm produces on average twice as much as one hour's work in Europe. Americans have used their productivity mainly to increase their consumption but partly to increase their free time. Many unions have achieved a right to a normal four weeks paid annual holiday for their members, and the number of people with four week holidays is growing fast. The working week for most Americans is forty hours, or less, though this does not apply to those who have senior positions in management, many of whom work very long hours indeed. In fact the people with the highest incomes have in general relatively small amounts of leisure compared with the people who have moderate incomes. For the rest, a thirty hour working week is not far away. Evidently, the problem of what is to be done with the ever increasing amount of leisure is occupying American sociologists a great deal. After all, until recent times, without a leisured class, Americans were too engrossed in work to bother about other things. 'Active occupation is . . . the principal source of their happiness . . . they are absolutely wretched without it'—so wrote F. J. Grund, a German commentator of the 1830s. In some ways American life is not particularly well adapted for the enjoyment of leisure; many of the things that people like to do in European countries are not really available to Americans. They cannot go and see cathedrals; they cannot spend summer evenings strolling up and down a *corso* in the Italian fashion. Their towns are just not designed for that purpose and in general the country is not easily accessible.

First of all Americans when they are free concern themselves with their homes and with their activities at home. Most people have an ambition to own their own house in a little piece of ground, and very large numbers of them have achieved that ambition. In this sense America is much more like England than it is like the rest of Europe, and round the large cities the houses spread immense distances from the centres.

Of all the new housing units started to be built in 1964 more than seventy per cent were in big cities or their suburbs, and three-fifths of the total were one-family houses. The figures show how, while more and more people are working in and around big cities, most prefer not to live in city conditions. Many new houses are built by speculative companies, which offer a choice between many types and price levels, yet including standardised parts. Houses are not excessively expensive in relation to their quality by European standards, and in relation to income levels they look very reasonable. Two-thirds of all families own the houses in which they live; the proportion is lower in the north-east where concentration in big cities leads to a higher proportion in blocks of rented flats (or apartment houses) on the European pattern. In some states the proportion is above three-quarters, though many of the owners have borrowed money on the security of their houses and their jobs in order to pay for them.

As the suburbs grow, so the city centres tend to become mainly places for business, and except in the biggest cities which are tourist attractions in themselves the central areas are losing commerce to the suburbs. In suburban areas shopping centres are being established, each a group of perhaps fifty shops around a huge car park; and the main unit of the shopping centre is usually the supermarket, typically on a scale far bigger than anything one can normally see in Europe— though similar places are appearing in Europe too. The modern American woman is accustomed to buying all her food in weekly visits to the supermarket, bringing it home in the car and storing it in the deep-freeze.

Once an American has reached his home he is interested in working to improve it and in making it as pleasant as possible. There is a strong incentive to spend much free time at home when the home is well-equipped, comfortable and attractive;

even the private swimming pool is no longer reserved for the very rich. One of the first activities at home is making things, mending things and working on the car. Apart from that there is television, and in most parts there are at least three programmes to choose from.

Americans invite their friends to their homes more than most people in Europe. Parties for children and for grown-ups are constantly occupying the leisure hours, usually with something to drink. In their new suburbs Americans are extremely friendly and hospitable. They are also very interested in each other, and when a new family moves into a suburban house the neighbours will be calling at once to see if they can help in any way. The problem of personal social barriers has been overcome very much more successfully than in any part of Europe, including England. So although each home may be a unit looking inwards to itself, it is also a unit which is much involved with the activites of the homes round about it. It is almost a tradition that there should be no fences or hedges between gardens. The new suburb recreates the sense of community of the old country village so that a family's home, instead of being an isolated island, is itself a part of a group of homes. It is possible to turn it into an island, but not many suburbanites want to do that. Most find their homes more satisfying because of their links with the neighbours—and also not too narrow because they still have plenty of contacts outside the neighbourhood. Most go to work in another place, so that the suburban home is only a part of their environment.

One thing that goes along with the gregariousness of American suburban home dwellers is a tendency to be much concerned with material possessions. It is quite true that the constant visits of friends and neighbours encourage many Americans to display their possessions and to show that they are as good as the possessions of their neighbours. It is not enough just to have the usual array of machines and gadgets in the house; they must be new ones and the best ones too. In this sense the gadgets which increase leisure act at the same time as an encouragement to more work and more earnings, and are sometimes regarded as ends in themselves, not merely as useful tools with which to avoid unpleasant work. The acquisition of the latest dishwashing machine is followed by the air-conditioning system, the swimming pool, the added sun-room or covered terrace.

But an American whose income rises as his career makes progress soon looks for a better house, in a better district, with more land, a better view, a bigger and finer swimming pool. He may be attached to the house which is his home for the time being but this does not imply that he has roots there. Today's job, today's income, today's home, today's friends and neigh-bourhood: all these are part of an American's (and his family's) identity. Instant coffee, instant friends—but nothing is regarded as permanent; the American hopes and expects to exchange them all for something better, and he finds no difficulty in identifying himself with the new.

Outside the home American towns do not provide very much in the way of public attractions for their inhabitants. And what they do provide is often arranged nowadays so that people sharing in a communal enjoyment still behave as though they were separate units. It was in America that the cinema first developed, but the average American now goes to a cinema only six or seven times a year, or less than half as frequently as the average Russian. Except in cold weather one way to see a film is to go to a 'drive-in movie', where you do not need to leave your car. An enormous screen is put up in an open space, and the cars are all parked facing the screen in long rows. When you have parked you open the car window and bring in the instrument which gives the sound, and perhaps a heater too. If it is cold you shut the window again, with the speaker inside the car so that you can hear while watching the big screen in front. Drive-in movies usually have some kind of café in the area, and dark figures glide between the cars to buy Coca-Cola and coffee to drink back in the car. It is curious that Americans have taken with such enthusiasm to this form of entertainment, because it is often supposed that one of the attractions of attendance at cinemas or other large gatherings is the satis-faction of being together with large numbers of other people in a single room; at a drive-in movie you have only the imagined company sitting in rows of dark cars round about. But a big car is very comfortable, and the young may like the privacy while the older can take the children with them. Babies can sleep on the back seat. And there is no need to bother about smart clothes.

Apart from the movies, towns offer bowling alleys and many facilities for sport, which are well used. But except in New York and a few other places people make very little use of the kind of urban life that is popular in European cities. In the average American town at nine or ten o'clock at night there is nobody to be seen in the central area (or 'down-town' section as Americans would call it) where the main shops and offices are. The offices are closed anyway and the down-town shopping areas are themselves no longer important centres of attraction, as so many Americans shop in the centres which have been specially constructed away from the middle of towns. There are bars and saloons, but they are generally not particularly attractive, and even in warm climates and in the summer it is not standard practice to arrange these with tables and chairs outside. The federal capital, Washington, was designed under the influence of Paris with wide avenues and immense amounts of spaces, but there are few open air cafés on the avenues. People do not use the pavements for strolling and looking around them, but only for the purpose of getting from place to place—or more often for getting from their car to some place where they have to be.

There are indeed plenty of restaurants, and they are good on the whole, although they may seem to be very like one another. Service tends to be better than in Europe and prices are reasonable. It is difficult to find a restaurant which is really cheap, but you are less likely to find excessively high prices in an American restaurant than in a European one.

The motor car is the great key to American life and amusement. Americans long ago became accustomed to their cars and use them enormously. The number of families that have two cars is already large and constantly growing. Father goes to work in one, mother uses the other for visiting friends, shopping, and carrying children. In a suburban family with one car, there are usually three effective possibilities: father is driven to his work by a friend, or mother takes him there, or he drives himself, leaving mother marooned. For a suburban family with no car at all life is very difficult, dependent on a long walk to the route of an unreliable, infrequent and expensive bus-service. In central parts of cities things are different.

Americans have an astonishing capacity for sitting inside

their cars for hours together, and the wish not to get out is catered for not only by such things as drive-in cinemas and churches, but also by drive-in banks and restaurant facilities, where you can do your business or get something to eat or drink through the window. It is partly because even ordinary cars are so big and comfortable that people like sitting in them and also because the roads are good, well-planned and adequate for the traffic.

The main discouragement to motoring in many areas is that there is nowhere much to go. Ordinary roads out of towns have a specially depressing ugliness. All over America they look alike, with the same wires, filling stations and advertisements showing in huge letters the wonderfully cheap prices of some goods or others. Even the affluent Americans are interested in 'ten cents off'. There are also interminable used-car lots with their rows of sad old cars, each with the price marked in enormous figures. The monotony of the roadside scene does not necessarily deter people from just getting in the car and driving.

Although there is not much informal free countryside, there are plenty of places which are organised as objectives for excursions: lakes with white-lined car-parking areas, cafés, landing-stages for boats and fishing, warning notices about things which are dangerous or forbidden. Some are privately developed, but the public authorities have been very successful in developing attractive places as county parks or state parks, and in the really spectacular regions there are the famous national parks which were pioneering arrangements of their kind. The greatest of all these are in the Rocky Mountains.

There are altogether about 2,000 areas designated as national, state or county parks in the United States. Some are quite small public areas centred upon some natural attraction, like the very obscure Hart Springs County Park in North Florida, where a natural spring makes a small lake of clear water. Round it are picnic tables scattered in the wood, places to make fires to cook food, shelters in case of rain, changing-rooms for swimmers, all quite free and with plenty of room to park cars. Very different is the Everglades National Park, near Miami in South Florida, a vast swampy area more than 100 kilometres from north to south and from east to west. Most visitors just drive across it on the main road, stopping to take a half-hour's

*Pop Art: Campbell's Soup by
Andy Warhol (1965)*

A futuristic shopping centre

trip into the swamp in a noisy flat-bottomed boat, failing to see the exotic birds which have wisely decided to move to quieter places. But more enterprising visitors go for long journeys into the wild parts of the swamp and find plenty to reward them. Every state has its parks both large and small, devised for long and short visits. Even so, in 1962 the Americans made on average just over one visit each to a park.

The smaller local county and state parks are generally very well arranged and provide very suitable facilities for outdoor enjoyment, whether inland or by the coast. Even the arrangements for simply stopping and having a picnic are very good, though always organised. Every main road has frequent picnic areas beside it in which it is easy to drive a little way from the road and stay for a short time or a long time in very pleasant surroundings. But in many regions it is not easy for people to make excursions to any part of the countryside that they choose. There are many public beaches on the coast, chosen, designated and equipped by some authority, but most of the coastline in the eastern and southern United States is either inaccessible or occupied by private property. Along much of the coast one can travel for long distances along a road 100 metres back from the coast but find the whole of the area between the road and the shore occupied by private houses. Everywhere the amount of private development along the shores of the sea and of lakes makes it difficult to gain access to water except at recognised places, many of which are organised as state or county parks.

Going for a walk, whether in town or in the country, is just not part of the American idea. An English journalist who was just walking along the road in Los Angeles was questioned by the police because it seemed so strange that he should be doing this. Except in town centres it is rare to find any side-walk beside a road, and some suburban roads are so bad that cars have to travel very slowly—too slowly to be dangerous to children. A person who tries to walk at night may find not only that he is almost spraining his ankle on the uneven surface, but also that there are no lights (the headlights of cars being good enough for the motorists) and that he will be pursued by angry dogs from the houses among which he is passing. The dogs are so unaccustomed to seeing anybody walking that, like the Los Angeles police, they think he must be up to no good.

Long journeys by road (often 800 kilometres in a day) are the basis of many holidays. The usual place to stay for the night is a motel. A few motels have been developed in Europe in recent years, but for a long time the motel has been a very important part of the American scene, responding to the wishes of people travelling long distances by car. There are traditional hotels in the main city central streets accessible to the railway stations and to travellers by air or bus, but they are not much use to motorists because parking near them is difficult and expensive, costing several dollars a day. People who travel by car usually spend their nights at motels by the roadside in the country, suburbs or small communities. There are certain traditions about the motels. Most have no upper floor, and the car can be parked just beside the bedroom. In a moment luggage and supplies can be moved into a small bungalow or suite of connected rooms, with private bath—and of course radio and television—the whole making a good family home for the night. Some even provide private kitchens. The motel-keepers put up prominent notices outside to tell passing travellers whether there are vacancies or not.

During a long day's journey in summer it is very tantalising to pass motel swimming pools by the roadside, inviting with their clear water and cool trees, but deserted because they are reserved for people staying the night and none are there in the daytime. During the long hot hours of the journey the traveller can look forward to a bathe in the pool at the motel where he will stay the next night, but he will not arrive until the cool evening.

Much of America is rich in inland water, and at weekends the rivers and lakes are full of an endless variety of boats; travelling fast or slowly, their owners looking for enjoyment through a form of movement older than the motor-roads. Boats are used for fishing, of course, but also just for travelling along for pleasure. Motor boats, many of them fast and noisy, often arouse bitter resentment among those who sail or paddle canoes more peacefully. In some areas long journeys are possible, and for those who have no cabins, or who want to sleep in comfort, there are botels, in which the characteristics of motels are pleasantly adapted for the water-traveller.

The attraction of boats lies partly in the chance they give of returning to a modern replica of the individual pioneer's simple life. The popular activities of fishing from boats or bridges, and shooting in the forests, are often surrounded with log cabins and other trappings which make the suburbanite at his weekend sport feel like a frontiersman.

Over most of the United States, even in the north, the summers are very hot, and the attractions of swimming are obvious. The possession of a private pool in the suburban yard or garden is now one of the near-universal ambitions of the ordinary family, and a family with an average income can usually provide itself with one. Every motel but the simplest has one—and the millions who live near the coasts have the sea, to say nothing of the inland lakes. Except for the few who have their homes on the shore, bathing in lake or sea is usually possible only from organised bathing places, in state or county parks, and not allowed when there is no lifeguard on duty. It is quite usual for the lifeguards to be withdrawn early in September, but even if the weather is hot most people accept that the season for bathing is over. They may not be convinced that all water is dangerous but the rigidity of the rules is little criticised. The great American ideal of freedom does not stop people from thinking that they should enjoy themselves in accepted and standardised ways, at what they are told are proper times and in proper places.

It has already been suggested that leisure pursuits tend to conform to various established patterns—not perhaps more so than in other societies, but more than one might expect in a society so individualistic. This is further illustrated by the fact that Americans tend to use much of their leisure in activities undertaken in the context of organised groups, both light-hearted and serious. Surveys have shown that the proportion who belong to societies is far greater than in Europe, and to many people things done in societies are exceedingly important. Some societies revolve round good work for the community, others round sport, others are cultural or social. Leadership is widely diffused, and an active member of a church, a rotary club, a parent-teachers association or of the League of Women Voters has a social role which gives significance to his or her life and place in the community, by this participation and identification.

All this social effort has contributed to a recent development which is making urban life more cultivated than it used to be. Apart from New York most towns were for a long time weak in music, theatre and the arts. By now the rest of the United States has gone so far in material development that it is no longer satisfied with being a cultural desert. Amateur orchestras and dramatic groups have flourished, taking their place among the manifold social activities—but these have also developed taste and talent. And more and more communities have developed music and the theatre in a more serious way. Where these things have not been developed commercially for profit local organisations have filled the gap; and as an increasing public has responded, so the theatre, less restrained by censorship, has become more lively and broadened its contribution to the discussion of social problems.

Americans participate in sport themselves probably rather more than people in Europe. Certainly those who participate succeed in developing a very high standard, as the success of Americans in international competition shows. The great majority have all the advantages of good living conditions and a more than adequate diet; the average height of young Americans has increased and is well above that of the European countries from which their ancestors orginally came.

America has developed some spectator sports of its own which are little practised elsewhere, in particular American football and baseball. Football is derived from the English game of rugby, which has been adopted in other English-speaking countries but only in a few parts of Europe (notably in south-western France). The American form requires very sophisticated equipment and considerable organisation. It is a game which cannot easily be adapted to a patch of empty ground where boys use coats for a goal. It is played at schools, but by its nature it tends to attract a rather restricted group of boys, and, as was explained in the chapter on education, normally played by those who hope to become serious players. Apart from the university teams there are many professional football teams, and they play in large stadia on Saturday afternoons, often before large crowds. The game is played with an oval ball; players may carry it and tackle each other (so that one player may throw another down as part of the game). The rules are

complicated, and the game is inherently dangerous. Many
players have been seriously injured or even killed in the past,
but in order to avoid such injuries the most elaborate protective
clothing has been developed. With dramatic protection for his
head, shoulders and chest, and a visor over his face, a player
when fully equipped looks like a ferocious and malevolent
visitor from another planet. The average football player looks
formidable enough in private life, with his close-cropped hair
and well-trained toughness, but a team of these armoured giants
looks frightening indeed.

A first class football game is played in the midst of an
immense ritual. Half an hour before the game begins bands
with majorettes begin marching and playing music on the field,
and their convolutions make the preparations in many ways
more interesting than the game itself. Supporters are urged to
cheer by cheer-leaders, who are normally girls wearing a
distinctive uniform. Thus the football game is not merely an
entertainment for the spectators but a pageant, using many of
the devices which are also employed in connection with political
rallies.

Association football, as played over all the rest of the world,
has been neglected and has only recently appeared as a sport
arousing much attention. But the isolation imposed on
American sport by its distinctive type of football not played
elsewhere, is likely to encourage the development of ordinary
football so that participation with other countries can be
extended.

Another winter game that is much played is basketball,
usually inside a large building. This too is accompanied by
special ritual performances, and is highly commercialised.

As a summer game the Americans have adapted the English
cricket to their own tastes in the form of baseball. This is a
much cruder and simpler game than cricket as played in
England, and resembles the game called rounders often played
elsewhere by children. Here too protective clothing is a part of
the performance, though except for the catcher it seems scarcely
as necessary as for the football players. Professional baseball
teams have enthusiastic followings, and important baseball
games arouse great interest, being followed on television all
across the nation. This is a large scale commercial enterprise,

bringing huge financial rewards to players and management alike.

Football and baseball are the two most distinctive American sports. Mention should also be made of golf, played mostly by the business community, and providing a useful basis for business contacts. There is a certain social importance in this game, and it is mainly organised in clubs whose members pay large fees.

In sport as well as most leisure activities we may notice two qualities which are rarely far away. One is commercialism. Pleasure is organised by people who make money out of it and so it may be expensive. A group of workers who had gained four weeks' annual paid holiday argued that their holiday pay should be at above normal rates, because their leisure cost so much. And when the pleasure seeker is not actually buying his amusement he is surrounded by advertisements and it is a little harder than in most of Europe to escape from this. The second quality of leisure pursuits is the togetherness of their followers. The noticeable stereotyping of pleasure in this individualistic society may seem paradoxical, but it is not difficult to find an explanation. American society lacks long-established social traditions and people follow current fashions out of a sense that what one is doing is valid because others are doing it too; whether or not the contact with others is obvious and immediate is not important. Another factor is that mass-market advertising promotes conformity in matters of taste.

CHAPTER ELEVEN

Communications

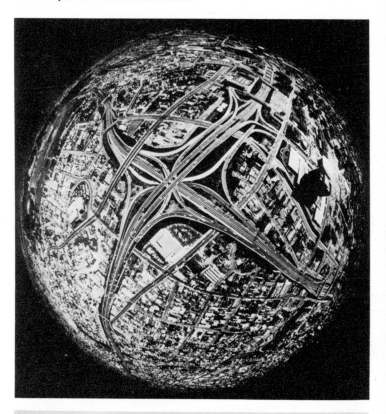

Road network in Los Angeles

Parked cars

1. Public Transport

With freedom of movement and trade over the whole of the United States the country depends to a great extent on its communications, both for moving people and goods and for conveying news and information from one place to another. The great·nation-wide companies and government agencies depend on effective links between offices and factories far apart from each other. Every kind of communication—transport, mails, telephones, radio, television, the press—affects every aspect of life and contributes to the cultural and economic uniformity which unites people of so many different origins living in so great an area.

As everywhere the simplest and least disturbing way of moving heavy loads, provided that there is no great hurry, is by water. All along the east coast the protected inland waters are amply used not only by private pleasure boats but by huge barges and other cargo vessels. West of the Appalachians many of the industrial centres, right across to the mid-west, are linked by the Ohio, Mississippi and Missouri river systems—though less colourfully now than in the romantic steamboat days; in the north, with the recent opening of the St Lawrence Seaway, a great joint project with the Canadians, ocean-going ships can (except when stopped by winter ice) sail right up through the Great Lakes to Chicago. For big consignments these waterways are linked with coastal shipping, and the Panama Canal is an important link between east and west. Here we come to a regrettable part of the story. American shipping costs are high, because the sailors must be paid on American scales and because mass-production methods have a limited value for

213

building the ships. If foreign ships were allowed to take part in the coastal trade they could do the work more cheaply. But, to protect the domestic shipbuilding and shipping interests, federal laws exclude all foreign operators from this service, and thus keep its costs high.

Railways are still important for carrying goods. They were built by private enterprise and though regulated by the Federal government they are still operated by commercial companies each of which operates only in part of the country—though companies run in competition between many of the important centres.

The railways have passed through great changes, and have more before them. In the development of the country in the last half of the nineteenth century, they completely transformed the conditions for opening up the west. Their huge steam-engines pulled trains across the continent, along tracks belonging to dozens of companies. In many cases two or more rival railways were built parallel with one another; even here competition has operated until very recently. Now there have been many amalgamations of railway companies, and the freight-trains compete against the mammoth trucks which roar along the roads, each one lit up at night like a Christmas tree. Some of the railway companies still manage to make a profit from their operations of carrying freight, but for a long time they have all lost money on their passenger services. Year by year, these services are reduced, and now, except for commuter lines around big cities, the passenger network has only a few routes still working. Even the New York Central is proposing to abandon its passenger train between New York and Chicago—a journey of 1,600 kilometres on which it cannot compete with airlines for speed or bus for cheapness. This is a matter for regret, because the long-distance passenger trains have a romantic history, with their famous names, such as the *Twentieth Century Limited,* and further west, across the continent from Chicago, the *Super Chief.* They progressed from the days of the old tourist sleeping cars and open observation platforms to the modern diesel-hauled towns on wheels, with club cars, drawing rooms and vista-domes, where passengers can sit on an upper deck by day to enjoy the scenery. The great long-distance trains moving east, west and south from their terminals in Chicago, have for long surpassed the trains of Europe in comfort. But each year fewer of them operate.

It is perhaps already too late to mention long-distance passenger trains as part of American life. Discussion of something so nearly extinct may seem like mere sentimental evocation of the past. In its latest form the long-distance train has a character which matches the journeys to be undertaken. As in Russia, the terms first and second class are formally avoided, being replaced not by 'soft' and 'hard' but by 'pullman' and 'coach'. The cheapest accommodation is in a coach, with comfortable tip-back seats all facing the same way. Even coaches have mens' and womens' 'rest rooms' which, to a European, look like improbable boudoirs or hairdressing saloons. In pullmans small compartments for one person are called roomettes. The larger compartments, for two people or for families, are called drawing rooms or bedroom suites, and the conversion from day to night use involves an elaborate and total transformation, carried out by the attendant, traditionally a Negro. A long train journey can have some of the quality of a cruise at sea.

For carrying people between big city centres and the suburbs there may be a new task for railways, or some other type of mass transport, in the future. They have, even now, to move huge numbers of commuters into town in the mornings and home again in the evenings—but this concentration of traffic in two short periods of each day makes the operation unprofitable. The New York suburban lines have had great difficulties for a long time, and their services have been harshly criticised. But if the suburban lines gave up, even more new roads into the cities would have to be built, and the authorities are helping the railways to keep going. Everywhere city planners are thinking about possible future development of monorails and other new types of alternative to the motor car for massive movement of people. All modern cities have similar problems, but the more widespread the suburbs the more difficult the problem becomes, and the American's preference for living far out of town, rather than in an apartment within the city area, makes the problem particularly difficult. The motor car has made this great spread possible, and has destroyed its older rival, but people are being forced to ask whether local railways

could be developed again for carrying people within metropolitan areas.

For long distance public transport of passengers as the
railways steadily withdraw, the traffic is now divided between
aeroplane and bus. Although distances are so great it is possible
to travel right across the United States by bus, and the Grey-
hound Bus Company even provides tickets for unlimited travel
all over the nation for a three months' period at the amazingly
low cost of a hundred dollars or so. Bus travel is cheap, and as
the roads are good enough to allow buses to travel fast, the time
spent on bus journeys is less than one might expect. With their
tip-back seats, and lavatories on the vehicles, the air-conditioned
buses are built to make all-night journeys as tolerable as
possible, and they have their clientèle.

Evidently the aeroplane has made great progress, and for
business travel and much private travel it seems the obvious
means to use. No other means can take a person across the
continent in six hours, and all major cities are joined to one
another by several companies competing with one another in
quality of service. All over the world airports are much like one
another, and their uniform pattern of ticket styles, checking-in
arrangements and lounges comes from American practice. Any
air-traveller within Europe may feel that his whole journey is
almost too American, and the air hostesses who smooth his
journey are fulfilling an essentially American role. All the
same, it would be quite wrong to give the impression that the
average American family goes off across the continent in a
plane as a matter of course. In 1966 only eighty million
individual passenger journeys were made by scheduled internal
trunk services and fifteen million by local services; when we
remember that thousands of executives and other top people
make twenty, fifty or a hundred journeys each by air in a year,
we should not be surprised to learn that more than half of all
Americans have never flown at all. This proportion is declining
rapidly. Within a few years the number of air travellers may
double, and if supersonic flight becomes available for internal
public services it will be possible to go across the continent for
a meeting and back within one day, provided that the planes
can land without delay. The most difficult immediate problem
is that of dealing with the great numbers of planes entering

and leaving the airports, and the new generation of jumbo jets, however unattractive they may seem, will be needed to cope with the ever-increasing number of passengers. Already by 1968 air travel between big cities was becoming strangled by the scale of its operations, with planes arriving at one of the New York airports obliged to spend up to two hours going round in circles in the air, waiting their turn to land. The absurdity of this, at the end of a journey covered at 1,000 kilometres an hour, makes people angry, but the solution, more airports, bigger planes, or both will not have much effect before 1975. Supersonic flight will not help this; it will only make the absurdity seem more absurd. Another solution would be for medium journeys, like Washington to New York, to go back on to the railways—but there is more talk about possible new surface transport in the future than action to make the existing railways effective competitors for the traffic.

2. The Motor Car

For most personal travel people use their own individual transport. Nothing is so expressive of the modern American way of life as the motor car, with the freedom of movement that it provides. It has been commonplace for so long that it has lost its novelty. Advertising and social pressure tell Americans that they must buy cars. Fortunately they want to; if they did not the whole economy would collapse.

One in seven of all workers makes cars or serves them. Up to eight million new cars are made each year; four households out of five own at least one car, and more than a quarter own two each. The minority without a car are mainly old people and inhabitants of crowded city-centres. There are over eighty million cars and fifteen million commercial vehicles (which Americans call 'trucks', not 'lorries').

In some western states there are already more than half as many cars as people. The poorest states such as Mississippi, Alabama and West Virginia have one car for every three and a half people, and the figure is about the same for New York State, brought down by the special conditions of New York City. In California there are almost twice as many cars as men; in the built-up area of Los Angeles alone three times as many

cars as in the whole of Sweden, which has about the same
population and the highest proportion of cars to people in
Europe. When Mr Khrushchev was shown some of the three
million cars of Los Angeles in 1959, moving (even then) five
abreast on the freeway he could see for himself how the
humblest worker had a possession reserved in Russia for the
greatest magnates; but his comment was 'What a waste!' And
indeed the spread-out suburban style of life, typified by Los
Angeles, is made possible by widespread car ownership and in
its turn makes public transport by bus or train an unsatisfactory
means of moving people between home, work, shops and social
activity. So it encourages people to want more cars. But the
cars of Los Angeles bring plenty of trouble; first the smog, a
kind of petrol-fume fog which for some years has polluted the
air and which only now is being attacked through the compulsory use of devices to consume the exhaust fumes; then the
insatiable need for more and more roads, more expenditure,
more damage to the environment. Los Angeles is already famous
for its motorways; in the next fifteen years 1,000 kilometres
more will have to be built, each for at least six lines of traffic.
Mr Khrushchev was not exactly wrong; but the people can
afford the cars and roads, and the situation which he criticised
was produced by free decisions of individuals and of a government chosen by the people, taking action (with their approval)
to satisfy the needs which they had created.

Not only in Los Angeles but all over America state and
federal authorities are now pouring out resources for improving
the road system. By 1960 the states were spending twice as
much on roads as they had done in 1950, and the general run
of expenditure for highways is now nearly ten times as much
in dollars as in 1930, although the proportion of cars to people
has only doubled in that period and the value of a dollar has
not declined to anything like the same extent. By the middle
1960s the total annual expenditure on roads in the United
States amounted to $11,000 million dollars, or $50 per person.
This is about four times as much as in England (which still
shows an exceptional parsimony in this matter) and twice as
much as in most European countries. Although Americans like
to keep control over their own personal expenditures and
personal freedom, they can see that if they want cars they must

have roads for the cars to use. The French and the British are only now beginning to see this. Part of the money for road development comes from the Federal government, which has enormously increased its participation in recent years. The federal contribution to road building in California was nearly twenty times as great in 1964 as it had been in 1950.

Every important city can now be entered and traversed by motorways with two, three or four lines of traffic on each side of the central division, and without any level junctions. Outside towns several long motorways were already in use by 1950, but an immense further increase in the system was then planned; 40,000 kilometres of new inter-state highways are by now in use, and by 1975 the total should reach 70,000 kilometres.

Although these roads have eliminated many of the sources of danger in the movement of traffic (no intersections, no people walking or slow moving vehicles) they are subject to strict regulations. Even on the motorways there is usually a speed limit of about 100 kilometres per hour, never more than 110. These speed limits are strictly enforced, and a driver who exceeds the speed limit is likely to pay a heavy fine. He may also have some black points marked on his licence, and if he gets too many black points he may have his licence taken away.

Americans have developed a rather mature attitude to the use of their cars. Although nearly all American-built cars can travel at over 150 kilometres per hour (and many of them at 200), most people are not enthusiastic about driving very fast, and do not regard their cars as a means of showing their daring and skill. Traffic discipline is well observed, and when drivers are ordered to keep in particular lines, they do not break out of their lines so as to pass others. Where there are are road intersections there are always clear indications as to which cars must stop, and traffic signals are provided much more liberally than in Europe. So the business of promoting safety through the design of the roads has been carried a long way, and drivers generally respect the rules. Americans who drive in Europe are horrified at the way the drivers behave, and some having hired a car return it after a few hours because they find the conditions intolerable.

It is only recently that great attention has been given to safety in the design of the cars themselves. The advertisements used to claim that cars were elegant, fast, economical to run, but did not remind people of the dangers of motoring by claiming that the cars were safe. In 1966 a campaign for greater attention to safety in the design of vehicles was launched with great effect. The manufacturers at first tried to find some way of discrediting the campaign, but soon they introduced new safety designs in their next models, and it seems that concentration on safety will now become a very important selling point.

Some Europeans suggest that roads in America are very dangerous. This is not quite fair. Traffic accidents kill 50,000 Americans every year, and this is indeed a little more than in Germany, France, Britain and Italy put together. One in fifty of Americans who die each year is killed on the roads (as compared with one in ninety in Britain); but in relation to the number of cars and the amount of movement the total is less than half of that in France or Germany. Considering how much of American traffic movement takes place in conditions of very great pressure, it seems that Americans have dealt with this terrible problem more effectively than the British, and much more so than the Germans, the Swiss, the Italians or the French.

In road safety there are big differences between states. More than twice as many people are killed, in relation to the number of vehicles on the roads, in Mississippi and Georgia as in Connecticut. Even in this matter the record of the south is far worse than that of the rest of the United States, and when one remembers that Connecticut and the other north-eastern states with favourable records are crowded, with high density of traffic, the difference looks even more discreditable to the south, where traffic-density is comparatively low. This is not because of bad roads in the south; on the contrary, in relation to the needs they are very good, and the south has a generous share of the new inter-state highway system. Safety on the north-eastern motorways has improved enormously in recent years, and they are probably the safest roads in the world. It looks as if the personal behaviour of drivers in New England is more civilised than in southern states, and very much more civilised than in Germany, Italy or some other countries of Western Europe.

Although the Federal government has recently paid part of the cost of building new roads, it has no power to regulate road traffic. Each state exercises sovereign power over its own roads, has its own system of taxation for cars and fuel and issues its own number plates, which are valid for one year only and serve as a receipt for the annual charge on the vehicle. Making car number plates is a traditional task of prisoners in state gaols.

Each state gives licences to drive to its own residents, and recognises licences issued by other states only for visits of restricted duration, just as it does with licences issued by foreign authorities. If an American moves to a new state he must pass its driving test (including questions on the state highway handbook) before he can get a licence. All states agree in having right-hand driving, but there are many differences in other ways. Each state has its overall speed limit, and people from Europe are surprised to find how low the limits are. Some states allow local communities to impose their own speed limits. Certain small towns deliberately fix unreasonable maximum speeds such as 40 kilometres per hour, where seventy would be perfectly reasonable, and collect much revenue through fines imposed on motorists from outside. In some cases the local policeman can collect the fines, and it has been known for one to disappear with his takings.

There was already one car for every five people forty years ago. The man who first saw and exploited the possibility of a mass production market for cars was Henry Ford, who has come to be identified with the whole modern industrial process. With his first mass produced Model T, he was notorious for saying, 'They can have any colour they like provided it's black.' But long ago Ford as well as its rivals moved a very long way from that position. The ordinary American car is bigger than even the largest of European cars, with few exceptions. It is high-powered and comfortable, and likely to be equipped with many luxurious devices, from automatic gear change to air-conditioning. If a car is a symbol of a person's status and wealth, it is the age of the car and its special equipment that indicates wealth rather than the fact that it is of a particular make. Everybody prefers to have an air-conditioned new car rather than an old one without special refinements. If a car has its windows shut in hot weather it is probably air-conditioned; but it may be that its owner is prepared to stifle in order that people may *think* he has air-conditioning even though he has not. Closed windows with no air-conditioning provide a cheap but uncomfortable phoney status symbol.

Sophisticated Americans are inclined to talk about cars as though they were a nuisance. Some people buy small European cars and thereby indicate their proud rejection of the standardised American product. They get some real advantage in busy town streets but none on the long trails through the endless country. Looked at in terms of status symbol a small European car is not only a sign of some capacity for individual choice, but a hint that its owner probably has a big one as well. But by now a second car in the family garage is being felt to be a tiresome necessity rather than a sign of opulence.

3. Posts and Telephones

Transport of people and goods represents only one aspect of communications. The transmission of information is another, in its way no less important. In twentieth century American communications we find one notorious contrast, that between the postal services and the telephones. The postal services, run by the central government, are always under attack—slow, expensive and irregular. The private enterprise telephones, on the other hand, are no less praised for their efficient, reasonably priced and courteous service. These popular images are not without foundation, though they are often exaggerated.

In having government responsibility for the mails the United States is following a universal practice among modern states. This is the only public service that has not been left to private enterprise, and the Post Office has always had a peculiar organisation. Its chief, the Postmaster-General, is a member of the President's Cabinet, and there is nothing unusual about this. But while most other Cabinet appointments are made with reference to ability rather than to party political considerations, it has been usual for a new President to give this office to his campaign manager or some party member who has been particularly helpful in the election. Local postmasterships have also been given on the recommendation of the state party organisation, working through their senators or congressmen.

These appointments have traditionally been important in the relations between the national administration and the state party machines. When the Post Office is so politicised there is not a good basis for efficiency. Apart from all this any postal service must have high costs in a society where the general level of wages is high because there is only limited scope for automatic processes. (In comparison with another labour-intensive service, hair-cutting, the postal service has kept its costs remarkably low in comparison with Europe.) The post-man's work in delivering letters is kept down by one very simple device. In streets where the houses are separate and standing well back from the road, each in its individual garden, the postman does not come to the door of each house, because each house has a mail-box of standard type by the roadway, designed so that the postman can put the letters in it without getting out of his car—and he can also collect outgoing mail.

The postman need have no difficulty in finding the houses where he is to deliver the letters—and strangers have little need to ask the way—as one thing that tends to be standardised, both in cities and in suburbs, is the system of numbering streets and houses. Some people may find this soulless, but it has some real advantages. A house with a name may sound very grand, but it is a trouble to the postman and to friends peering from house to house on a dark night, and American habits prefer convenience. If you have to go to a house in a strange place, and the address is 2240 North West Thirty-fifth Street, you can find your way straight to it without a map and without asking the way. The number 2240 does not mean that it is the 2240th house in the street. The number is really a kind of map reference, indicating that on North West Thirty-fifth Street it is two-fifths of the way between the twenty-second and twenty-third roads (or 'avenues') that cross Thirty-fifth Street at right angles.

This American method of numbering usually starts from two main roads crossing one another in the town centre; the north-south roads may be called 'streets' and those running east-west 'avenues', with the number of each house determined by its position. Fortunately there has to be provision for roads which curve, or otherwise depart from the rigid gridiron pattern, and for these names like 'terrace' can be used. Sometimes the system can be simplified if there is a barrier such as a big river to one side. So Manhattan Island in New York City does not need to bother with east and west. First Avenue is the first north-south road running down the east side of the island, and First Street crosses the island just at the northern boundary of the area of earliest settlement, where the streets were given names before the rationalisation was thought of. Even without names the streets can have their character: Fifth Avenue means as much as Oxford Street or Champs Elysées, Forty-second Street as much as Kurfurstendamm.

In a few towns, anxious to get away from the soullessness of numbers, streets are called by names so that the first begins with A, the second with B, and so on—but strangers have to learn how to work the system. This standardisation does not strike Americans as rigid or inappropriate. After all, much of the northern frontier of their country is along an artificial straight line, the forty-ninth parallel of latitude, and many state, county and city boundaries follow straight lines too. These are some of the signs that American man, in building a new society, new towns and political units, could already see where he was going.

The telephone was first developed on a substantial scale in the United States. Alexander Graham Bell, born and educated in Scotland, moved first to Canada in 1870, and in 1873 became a professor of vocal physiology at Boston University, where he made great contributions to aids for the deaf. He was one among many who were experimenting with the possibility of transmitting speech by wire. In 1876 he successfully transmitted a complete sentence by wire to a nearby room; and in due course, after prolonged litigation, he successfully established his claim to be the inventor of the telephone. A commercial switchboard was established· with twenty-one subscribers, at New Haven, Connecticut, in 1878, and within ten years the Bell telephone system had been brought into operation in many places.

Telephones were developed quickly by private enterprise, and as long ago as 1925 there were seventeen million telephones in use, and half of all households had telephones forty years before some major European countries. By now there are few households without one, and some have two separate connections to the system, because teenage children spend so long talking to their unseen friends that a single connection is not enough.

4. Radio, Television and the Press

After the telephone came radio, soon to be used for many purposes, including police work in hunting criminals and controlling traffic. The first radio programmes were put out by the manufacturers of equipment, to make it attractive to people to buy sets, but soon, in the 1920s, firms began to use radio for advertising goods they wanted to sell, and the advertisers themselves sponsored the programmes. This practice soon became firmly established, and was used for television too when this became generally available. Now there are several competing networks on both sound radio and television, with advertisers sponsoring the programmes. There is regulation through the Federal Communications Commission, established in 1934, but when those who put out the programmes have the aim of attracting as listeners or viewers the largest number of potential purchasers there is no escape from the dictates of popular taste. The result is rather monotonous, with many variety shows, give-away programmes and other types of light entertainment. It is not only the triviality that brings complaints. There is no formal censorship, but while in practice severe restraints are imposed on anything that might offend respectable feelings in matters of sex, the portrayal of crime and violence for entertainment and thrills goes on without restriction. Danger and excitement attract big audiences, and night after night handsome, virile, daring men go through their routines of fighting, shooting, menacing, deceiving and robbing. The wrong-doers may be caught in the end, but in conditions that make their actions look strong, their relation with society seems not a miserable social problem but an heroic contest, in which they just miss the most glittering prizes of wealth and power. Up to this point they are shown as having qualities worthy of imitation, and their crime has brought them luxurious homes and swimming-pools, cars and boats, not to mention the admiration of desirable girls and the respect of the operators of smart night-clubs and hotels. And if they are punished at the end, their punishment is retribution, imposed by a society which has been stronger than them in the use of the same tools, not a restriction imposed with regret on persons who have pursued their own advantage in an anti-social way. The public like to be excited, and as the sponsor must attract viewers in competition with rivals, his thrills must be more daring than his rival's thrills.

Western Europe has regarded the American experience as an example of what should not be done, and Americans who care for good standards of culture and taste have for long been deeply critical of the enslavement of the mass media to the business of selling. The stream of criticism has had some effect, and at the same time, as the rising generations are more highly educated, public taste has come to be less satisfied with triviality and excitement. The programmes do have room for news and political discussion, press conferences, even congressional hearings—but these are themselves greatly affected in their character by the fact that they are seen by millions.

In recent years new agencies, apart from the commercial networks, have entered these fields. Many universities operate radio and television stations, and in the San Francisco area there is a radio station financed by voluntary subscription broadcasting cultural programmes, lectures and discussions which is free from the demands of timetabling, and from the need to be sure of always giving equal time to the spokesman of each point of view.

Obviously the press is an important means of communication, and its function is taken very seriously. Many universities provide courses in journalism, and the journalist is usually a graduate with special training in the duties of the newspaperman to inform the public, to offer reasoned argument and comment without distortion of facts, to offer honest guidance. Many European popular papers arouse disapproval across the Atlantic. All the same, American newspapers tend to be rather dull. Their total daily sales, in relation to the population, are higher than in most of western Europe, but lower than in Britain. Because the country is so large, no single newspaper can compete on a nation-wide basis against local products; in many states it is very difficult to buy any newspaper from outside that state. With the press fragmented by zones, no newspaper has developed a circulation on the scale of the mass

A news-vendor in New York

newspapers of Britain and (now) of Western Germany. The nearest thing to a national newspaper is the *New York Times,* which is sold all over the United States, but in general only to people who may be considered to be of the élite. The newspaper is heavy and has to be carried by air if it is not to be hopelessly out of date, and this means of transport is inevitably expensive. It costs as much to buy a *New York Times* in Florida as to buy the London *Times.* The *Washington Post* is another paper often quoted, but it cannot be regarded as a single means of expression covering the nation as a whole.

Because most newspapers are sold only within a geographically restricted market they tend to concentrate on affairs that are of interest to their local readers. International affairs are reported but not very extensively, and the concentration on local affairs is responsible for the comparative dullness which strikes many foreign readers. It is not that American newspapers are insubstantial. Indeed they have far more pages than their equivalents in other countries, and the *New York Times* Sunday edition is well known for its bulk; over 200 pages, including many supplements. All substantial newspapers have enormous Sunday editions of this kind. Such great bulk is almost repellent. It is obviously impossible to read it all, and the task of selecting what is interesting tends to put the reader off.

Considering the high degree of training and dedication of American journalists one thing that we do find is a high sense of responsibility in putting over a balanced view in reporting. Some principles of journalism are very widely respected, such as separation of information from comment, and an insistence that views must be fairly stated without intention to mislead. Some columnists gain reputations surpassing those of all but a few politicians, and have great influence.

The press in America is particularly important because, more than in any other country, it is recognised as having a responsible role to perform in relation to one aspect of the process of government. The press conference is an American invention, and it began to be important in the form of a meeting between President and journalists in which the President replied to questions. Press conferences take place all over the world now, but the presidential press conference is an institution which gives us a key to the special role America assigns to the Press

and to the newspapermen. The British parliament has its
question time when each day members of Parliament address
questions to ministers in charge of executive departments, and
some European parliaments have something of the same kind.
There is no possibility of such a device in the United States
Congress because heads of executive departments are not
members of it. Thus the executive has no political platform
through which to expound its views and give information.
President Franklin Roosevelt showed the advantages of using
the Press for such purposes when he called regular meetings of
newspapermen at which he invited questions and gave information. This device is still regularly used, and although the
Press has no formally recognised role one cannot give a broad
picture of the American governmental process without
mentioning the part that the Press has to play in its contacts
with the President. A newspaperman attending the presidential
press conference is there not just as an employee of the newspaper for which he works, but as a representative of the
American public entrusted with the task of conveying information; his role in doing this has a real significance in the
democratic political process. The same could be said of press
conferences involving heads of departments or visiting foreign
statesmen or people in the news. The American scene would be
unimaginable without these occasions. The press conference
has become an institution and an indispensable element in the
whole system of public communication.

The American newspaperman's public responsibility goes
beyond the reporting of political facts, beyond even comment
on the facts. His role becomes heroic when he discovers crimes
about which the police knew nothing, and more still when he
produces evidence of corruption or misbehaviour by police
officials. However democratic the electoral process there have
been many local officials who have made themselves rich by
scandalous means, and a journalist who finds out the discreditable truth, relentlessly pressing his inquiries and
courageously publishing the results in the face of wicked
menaces, like David confronting Goliath, expresses one of the
highest ideals that the Press sets before itself. Things do not
always happen this way, but they sometimes do. And the Press
as a whole deserves some credit for the marvellous openness of

public life, which is one of the special features of American democracy. Many things which in other countries are hidden away are quickly made known in America. That this is so is partly due to the dedication of the Press to its task, together with the prestige that it has earned as a protector of the public interest.

CHAPTER TWELVE

America and the World

Astronaut Edwin Aldrin on the moon,
July 1969

Marines in Vietnam

The position of the United States in international affairs has
been largely transformed in the last two generations. Before
1914 the main objective of most Americans was to have as little
as possible to do with the troubles of the world outside. After
all, one motive in going to America in the first place was to
escape from the effects of the international conflicts and
revolutions in Europe. During the period when European
countries were competing for colonies the United States stayed
out of the contest. Its own colonial past, war of independence
and liberation had a lasting influence on policy. American
opinion has always tended to disapprove of colonial operations,
and has welcomed the processes in recent years by which most
of the European colonial powers have handed over independence
to their former overseas territories.

Before 1914 there were some sectional differences in attitudes
to foreign affairs. People who still had links with European
countries sympathised with their country of origin. Apart from
this, the mid-west, being further removed from the coasts and
thus from immediate international contacts, was somewhat
more isolationist, while the south favoured international
contacts. In our own time these differences have largely disappeared. The proportion of Americans with close memories of
their foreign backgrounds has declined, and developments in
communications have meant that the mid-west is no longer
more isolated from the rest of the world than the coastal regions.

The main factor in changing the approach to foreign affairs
has been the increase in American strength. The United States
wanted to stay out of the war of 1914, but at last they were

drawn into it in a mood of idealistic enthusiasm. It is significant that it was the American President, Wilson, who enunciated the fourteen points as a contribution to the ending of the war and to the settlement of affairs after it was over. His plan excluded the use of victory for national gain, and the idea of forming a League of Nations was in part to be attributed to his ideals. Almost all opinion supported him in seeking no rewards of victory, but when the war was over a new mood of isolationism soon gained strength, so that most Americans wanted to return to their former role without foreign commitments. The Senate gave expression to this mood when it failed to give its approval by the necessary majority to the signing of the Treaty of Versailles and American participation in the League.

Hitler's war produced something like a repetition of the former story. At this time the great majority of American opinion felt a revulsion against the objectives and methods of the Nazi government in Germany, but opinion was not in favour of Americans entering the war at the beginning. However there was enough sympathy for those opposed to Hitler for President Roosevelt to be able to receive public support in adopting a posture which was by no means neutral; the United States, in spite of its technical neutrality, gave help to Britain during 1940–41. When the Japanese attacked Pearl Harbour and the United States entered the war it was again without any purpose of making gains in terms of the world balance of power. This time America seemed itself to be in danger from two aggressive nations bent on conquest. But idealism was again a major factor in this struggle: idealism in support of democratic processes and against dictatorship.

American attitudes have always been against ideologies of every kind, and both fascism and communism have been rejected by the great majority of American people at all stages of history. So too in 1945 American opinion was in favour of a settlement which would secure peace rather than American domination. The United States for a time was placed in a position in which it could have dominated the world, but it made no attempt to do so. Far from it: for the first year after the ending of the war American government was supported by public opinion in the hope that reasonable arrangements could be made, and that these arrangements should include co-operation with all former allies, including Russia, in rebuilding a peaceful world.

During the war the United States had poured out resources in support of the Russian war effort. A flow of American materials had been sent to the Russians at immense cost for them to use in the operations against Nazi Germany. For this help the Americans received no thanks. The Russian public was scarcely informed about the dependence of their own war effort on the supplies of material of every kind which the Americans poured into their hands. Although this lack of response was hurtful, Americans were prepared to continue with their co-operation rather than nurse a grievance.

It became clear however that the Russians were intent upon extending their own power, especially in eastern Europe. In America the idealistic mood of the first post-war years soon gave way to one of deep bitterness and resentment towards the Russians and towards communism in particular. As an ideology communism was always hateful to the great majority of Americans, and it had required a great effort of will to be prepared to give so much help to the Russian communist régime in fighting a common enemy. When the reactions of the Russians were really understood, all the deep-seated hatred of communism in America soon reappeared.

The period of disillusion about the Russians lasted from about 1946 to 1949. But these were also years of imaginative and generous actions towards the rest of the world. During this period, while Harry S. Truman was President, the Secretary of State, George Marshall, put into operation the Marshall Plan of assistance to European countries devastated by the war. This assistance was offered to any who cared to take it, but in eastern Europe under Russian domination it was rejected. So the assistance was concentrated on western Europe, and linked with a scheme for co-operation among the nations of the non-communist world, including West Germany, in rehabilitating themselves. This scheme inevitably included a firm intention to oppose the further spread of communism into Europe. It was the Russians who were responsible for creating an Iron Curtain in Europe at that time, and the Americans responded with a determination that the Iron Curtain, though regretfully accepted, should not move further westwards.

Along with the Marshall Plan came the establishment of the North Atlantic Treaty Organisation, by which the United States and the western countries of Europe agreed to co-operate in international affairs. This plan won large consent in the United States and was accepted by majority opinion among all sections of society and in all parts of the country. Inevitably the plan included a measure of adherence to a doctrine of self-preservation and of the protection of national interests in the face of a menace whose existence was undeniable.

Since 1945 there has been an essential consensus of opinion among the American public about the main lines of foreign relations, but with considerable variations of view about particular matters. From the time when the Iron Curtain was placed across Europe there has been very wide agreement that communism should be contained, by force if necessary. Most Americans have been prepared to make sacrifices in defence of western Europe and for the sake of preventing communist régimes from spreading. In some ways the situation during Stalin's lifetime provided a sounder basis for this consensus than the developments since Stalin's death. When Stalin was alive it was perfectly clear that communist aggression could be contained only by a sufficient show of potential force to make it manifestly not worth while for military aggression to take place. Americans were reasonably confident of their military capacity backed by the atomic bomb.

Since Stalin's death the situation has been complicated. Nuclear power developed in the Soviet Union soon gave the Soviet Union the power to destroy the United States as effectively as the United States could destroy the Soviet Union. American opinion became aware of this, and rather than be concerned merely with containment it was ready to find ways of co-existence with communists under a precarious balance. Meanwhile the new régime in the Soviet Union, first under Khrushchev and then under his successors, offered hope for a return to a degree of positive co-operation between the world's two greatest powers. All this involved some reappraisal of feeling within the United States. The best hope for peace and security seemed to lie in the maintenance of the established spheres of influence of the two great powers, together with avoidance of positive extensions of influence by either. Because of this it is easy to see why Americans were ready to accept the acts of the Russians in Hungary in 1956 and in Czechoslovakia in 1968. Because of this too, there has been a special insistence that the Russians should keep out of the whole American continent. The violent antipathy to communists within the United States is easily understandable, although the American Communist Party has never been strong enough to be of any real importance; however the communist label can easily be attached to all kinds of malcontents and subversives, and indeed to any who question the established social values.

Resentment over the installation of a communist government in Cuba was extremely bitter. President Kennedy was following the well-known wishes of public opinion when he gave support to Cuban exiles in the hope that they might overthrow the Castro régime. It was only after the missile crisis of 1962 that American opinion began to feel readier to accept the Cuban situation. At least that affair seemed to have established that Cuba was not to become a Russian nuclear base. But it also left Americans anxious about the security of the continent as a whole. Any sign of a move towards a communist system in any of the states of Central and South America is seen as a direct threat to American security. Thus in spite of the democratic idealism which forms the fundamental aspirations of Americans there is a tendency to support any régime, however oppressive and unjust, so long as it is not communist. It is generally for this reason that America's reputation in the world has become identified with imperialism. Not surprisingly the communists are quick to exploit any possibility of representing the United States as an upholder of ancient and evil privilege against the mass movement of people for justice.

American attitudes to Africa and Asia have been influenced by two contrary emotions. There has been sympathy for the moves towards independence of the peoples who were formerly under colonial rule. Such sympathy arises out of the whole American experience and system of values. After all, the United States itself, long ago, led the way in liberation from colonial power, and the nation's whole history is tied up with the defence of independence. But sympathy with African and Asian aspirations, and readiness to spend resources in helping economic development, are mixed with fear of the spread of communism, whether spontaneously or through infiltration or subversion from outside.

During the period of the growth of new independent states. American governments were identified above all with maintaining order and stability, and were thus sympathetic to the already existing régimes, so long as they were not communist. This unfortunately encouraged support for régimes whose characteristics included some of those which had been so detested when they showed themselves in Nazi Germany. There was a deficiency of understanding about the aspirations of many peoples to be freed from the tyrannies which oppressed them. There was a lack of sympathy with the grievances of peoples in backward countries where wealth was concentrated in the hands of a few. Americans, aware that poverty affected only a small part of the people at home, tended to see society in terms of the competitive activity of individuals. In America there were differences of wealth, but for most of the population these differences did not involve poverty. The war and the economic policies followed at home after 1945 seemed to have removed the insecurity of the 1930s. From 1945 onwards the vast majority of Americans had secure and reasonable jobs, and had no need to fear poverty of the sort which afflicted so many only fifteen years before. From such a starting point it was not easy to understand the position of the majority of the peoples of Latin America and Africa. International contacts were largely with the tiny minorities of these countries who had succeeded in attaining wealth, while for the Americans the masses suffering from povery were faceless and voiceless. Thus there was a deficiency of sympathy towards the movements in favour of greater equality in the distribution of property.

In China the United States had co-operated with Chiang-Kai-Shek's nationalist régime, and failed to understand the forces that led to its eventual overthrow by communists in 1949. Coming on top of the Russian domination of eastern Europe, the capture of China by the communists was particularly disappointing. American reaction was from the first a determination that communism should be contained in the Far East as well as in Europe. With the shock of the communist victory in China went a feeling that all the Far East was in danger of coming under communist domination just as eastern Europe had done. So the doctrine of containment took charge, with somewhat unfortunate results.

After China was taken over by a communist régime there were two breaches in the primary assumptions of containment, though these were with difficulty accepted. Until 1950 a non-communist régime held power in Korea; the outcome of the Korean war, after great expenditure of men and resources, was to leave the northern part of Korea in communist hands, with the line of containment half-way down the country.

Meanwhile in Vietnam (or former French Indo-China) the French were having difficulties with attempts to prevent the installation of a communist régime in that country. In this case the Americans were not directly involved, but the 1954 settlement seemed to them to embody the final permissible concession to communist advance. There was an international guarantee of the arrangements made by which the southern part of the country had a régime based on some kind of democratic electoral system. From the beginning the communists continued their agitations in the southern part of Vietnam, and when the South Vietnamese government appealed to the Americans for help in dealing with what they regarded as communist insurrection within their own territory, the American government was ready to give that help. Public opinion supported it in doing so. The doctrine at this stage was 'so far and no further'. It was assumed that if the whole of Vietnam including the south became communist, communism would move on to take control in the next country and then the next. American opinion was ready to accept some sacrifices to prevent this from happening; it favoured and supported assistance to the South Vietnam government in the form of money and materials, and advisers; then finally even military forces. The American involvement increased steadily until by 1964 the operations on behalf of the South Vietnamese government against communist insurgents within the country had assumed the proportions of a regular war. The participation of forces sent over from North Vietnam produced an actual confrontation between forces of a communist régime and American forces. By 1968 the war had developed to such an extent that it was already the major preoccupation of the American government and of public opinion, involving vast expenditures of materials and over

500,000 American troops. All this seemed to produce very little result. In 1968 most of South Vietnam was in practice controlled by communists with aid from North Vietnam.

American opinion could justifiably feel aggrieved at the way the Vietnam war turned out. In the language of the communists in Russia and elsewhere the Americans were in South Vietnam as aggressors, and the term 'American aggression' became common currency throughout the world. Aggression is always difficult to define, but from the legal point of view it could justifiably be argued that if there were any aggressors they were the North Vietnamese who were sending military forces into the territory of another state. But Americans repeated this argument in vain, as far as world opinion was concerned. In their attempt to make their intervention effective the American forces made extensive use of terrible weapons of destruction, and the world came to identify American policy with the burning and destruction of people and villages, so that it became easier to attach to it the label of 'aggression'.

American reputation throughout the world suffered daily from the involvement in this war, and there was no hope of any profit coming from it. By 1968 it had become clear that the involvement was unlikely to produce results except continuing damage to the country America was trying to help and misery for its people; the reaction at home was for 'hawks'—supporters of a further extension of the war—to be ranged against 'doves' —those in favour of peace. Impatience with the costly stalemate led to increasing dissension. In the spring of 1968 opinion polls showed that about one-third of Americans were in favour of withdrawal even if this involved a loss of the position which the Americans had originally sworn to defend. Another one-third were in favour of more energetic measures to ensure victory. Another one-third were roughly in favour of the action currently being taken by the government. President Johnson's decision not to attempt to be elected President again coincided with his recognition of the need to modify existing policy. The early stages of the 1968 presidential election campaign were fought under the influence of arguments about exactly what the United States should do in order to bring the war to an end. Yet in the long run the two main contenders in the election did not seem far apart, either from each other or from President

Johnson, in policy with regard to the war. Opinions which had been opposing one another in peaceful and bellicose attitudes were confused by the beginning of negotiations in Paris, and rival views about the war seem to have had little clear effect on the election itself. All the same, foreign affairs had come to play a more important part in American politics than ever before.

During the past twenty years or so opinion poll organisations have been active in finding information about the degree of interest among the public in questions of foreign affairs. They have found that with the increased role of America in world politics a much larger section of the public takes the trouble to inform itself and to discuss international problems. Before 1945 there were periods in which only one person in ten considered foreign affairs as the most important problem facing the United States, yet when there was a special crisis the proportion could rise to two out of three. In the past few years the proportion thinking foreign affairs the most important problem has been much more consistent, so that we may say that there is a much more lasting sense of responsibility and involvement than in the past. As one might expect, the surveys show that people with more education (who on the whole are also those with higher incomes) tend to be more concerned with foreign affairs and more knowledgeable about them, and to have a greater consciousness of America's role in the world.

The dominant attitude has never changed from one of desiring peace above anything else. This has been accompanied by an aspiration to see the United Nations work as an effective institution, together with regret for its manifest failures. But the fear of communism has been a dominating influence and to some extent has counteracted the old idealism. Desire for peace is matched by a sense that America is in permanent competition with the communist world. When it became clear that the Soviet Union had a military capacity about equal to that of the United States a strong reaction followed. In particular the launching of the Russian sputnik led to a readiness for greatly increased expenditure not only for defence but for science and technology upon which the defence capacity must be based. While in the past Americans might wish to keep themselves free of foreign entanglements, now the sense of competition with the communist world is probably a more influential factor than the old peaceful idealism. At the same time, every sign of a possibility of co-existence with the communist world is now generally welcomed. This does not involve a sympathy with communism or its aims, but rather a recognition that without such co-existence the prospects for the continuation of peaceful life must be very poor. There is a readiness to recognise that a balance of power based upon spheres of influence may be the most effective means of preventing a disastrous conflict. Thus there may be a wish to maintain the status quo, and a fear of any new development which may threaten it.

The view commonly held of America is somewhat paradoxical. To people in developing countries Americans seem to be the successors of the old imperialists, whereas in the Americans' own eyes they are in fact no more than resisters of the communist drift. The positive aims of American policy are now expressed mainly in the form of technical assistance and financial help of every kind to the developing countries. Some may claim that motive is wholly selfish, concerned with holding back communism and maintaining the advantages of a rich country in developing markets. Like most prejudices this one is not entirely without foundation, but American opinion would not be ready to agree to the expenditure of a dollar a week for every family on aid to the rest of the world if there were not also a humanitarian motive. There may be impatience with the failure of the developing countries to reform their agricultural systems or to use the aid which they receive in the most effective way; but there is enough of the old idealism left for most of public opinion to feel that with its wealth America has a duty to try to help those parts of the world in which poverty is still the most serious problem. This involvement is more a moral one than a stabilising or a political one, at least as most Americans see it. In this sense there is a feeling that America, having been so successful in building up its own prosperity, has a mission to try to help others to follow in the same direction. However narrow and selfish this objective may be made to appear, in the long run it is, more than anything, an expression of a national generosity such as has not been seen before. To this extent America is being true to the ideals of its original foundation.

Index

(Note: 'ff' after a number means that this is the first of several pages relating to this subject.)

151-1198 69/05

C A N

Seattle

WASHINGTON

Portland
Oregon

COLUMBIA R.

MISSOURI RIVER

NORTH

MONTANA

DAKOTA

CASCADE

OREGON

IDAHO

SOUTH

DAKOTA

MT. SIERRA NEVADA

CALI-FORNIA

NEVADA

WYOMING

ROCKY

MOUNTAINS

NEBRASKA

San Francisco

UTAH

COLORADO RIVER

COLORADO

KANS

Los Angeles

ARIZONA

NEW MEXICO

OKLA

RED RIVER

Dall

TEXAS

PACIFIC OCEAN

MEXICO

HB